Catholic Theology
Facing the Future

Historical Perspectives

Edited by
Dermot A. Lane

THE COLUMBA PRESS

Knock
18/4/04

First published in 2003 by
THE COLUMBA PRESS
55A Spruce Avenue
Stillorgan Industrial Park
Blackrock, Co. Dublin
in association with Paulist Press,
Mahwah, New Jersey

Book design by Theresa M. Sparacio
Cover design by Valerie Petro

Printed in the United States of America

ISBN 1-85607-397-1

Contents

CONCLUDING REFLECTIONS

Dedicated in gratitude to the living memory of
Elizabeth A. Rafoul,
who was born in 1935,
graduated from the Graduate Program in Theology and Pastoral
Ministry at St. Michael's College, 1977, served as Administrative
Assistant to the Director of the Program from 1977 to 1992,
and died on 11 January 2000

AND

Reverend Dr. Paul Couture, SSE,
co-founder of the Graduate Program in the early 1960s,
Director of the Program from 1971 to 1992,
and currently Professor Emeritus at St. Michael's College,
Colchester, Vermont

Foreword

This is not a customary audience for a president of St. Michael's College. It is a rather unique occasion. Not too often do I have the opportunity to address a distinguished group of alumni who at the same time are a distinguished group of teachers and students of theology.

Theology and particularly the study of theology takes prominent place at our institution and even though at times the size may be somewhat inconspicuous, the impact and meaning are of substance and importance to St. Michael's College.

Last year, I had the opportunity to welcome the graduate students in theology to the summer school. At that time I was courageous enough to point them to some of their responsibilities. I will look for that same courage right now for the few observations I have been asked to make.

The German philosopher Heidegger made a wonderful distinction between *grund-probleme* and *grenz-probleme,* by which he sought to enlighten us about matters of gradual importance. I have used this image of *grund-probleme* and *grenz-probleme* in several settings, not in the least in explaining the real task and pursuits of a liberal education. But what is true in a liberal education is even truer for theology. The distinction by Heidegger invites theologians either to study, restudy, and revisit the classical perennial problems or to move to new horizons, new insights, new discoveries. In other words, we can focus in liberal education or theology on the fundamental problems—on the trunk of the tree—or we can explore and discover new insights, new fields of endeavor; we can cross boundaries, or, to use the tree metaphor, we can go out on a limb. That is what I believe contemporary theologians, particularly within the Roman church and especially within the academies of the Roman church, ought to do.

I have several concerns regarding the role, the task, and the responsibilities of theologians in our Catholic colleges and universities. I would plead with them to make it a clear-cut purpose to address the other academicians in our institutions and not one another. To state it differently: In addition to addressing one another, please spend equal time in addressing the other disciplines, the other academicians, the other academies. In the latest developments surrounding the implementation of *Ex corde ecclesiae*, one of the side effects may be, unfortunately, that theologians once again will be more tempted to address the bishops and the curia, the canon lawyers and regulations, rather than addressing the *grenz-probleme* and the problems created by the other academic disciplines.

It would be my hope that all theologians, without exception—whether dogmatic, scriptural, ecclesial, historical, or other—would dare follow the example of the wonderful exchange between the author Umberto Eco and Cardinal Martini. This dialogue, recently published as *Belief or Nonbelief?: A Confrontation* (New York: Continuum, 2000)—a book I recommend to all—should be an inspiration for theologians to address substantive issues with other academicians, with other faiths, with the secular world. We need in our time a resurgence of theologians who enjoy the freedom and the width and depth of knowledge as represented by Aquinas and Teilhard de Chardin. We certainly need new Aquinases and new Teilhards. In a fairly recent address the theologian Edward Schillebeeckx talked about the importance of moving boundaries; not removing, but the moving, the stretching in a certain sense, the dislocation of boundaries in order to achieve real results. Theologians, in dialogue with one another and with other academic disciplines, will be able to pursue deeper and wider issues. And, as a result of the questions raised by others, they will make new discoveries, and it is in discovery that they will advance the teachings of the church and the human spirit. It is discovery, not confirmation, that is more in line with the unfolding history of salvation. Theologians, particularly those in the academy, should always look forward to the tension between reason and faith. And should welcome it.

I certainly hope that St. Michael's College can be one environment in which this challenge is displayed before all. Not only the Catholics within our community but all members of our community should be struggling with these very issues. Hopefully your days together will advance the spirit in which this must happen. Thank you for your presence here at our college.

—MARK VANDERHEYDEN

Introduction

From 15 to 19 July 2000 St. Michael's College, Vermont, celebrated forty years of graduate theology and pastoral ministry in its summer school program. The college brought together into a four-day conference one hundred and fifty people: students, graduates, and faculty. The spirit of the conference was captured under the rubric of "Reunion 2000"—an international gathering of people who wanted to renew old acquaintances, replenish the wellsprings of Christian ministry, and look to the future with a sense of purpose. Following the well-established pattern of summer schools at St. Michael's College, there was throughout the conference a balanced mix of time for theological reflection and personal renewal, prayer and liturgical celebration, relaxation and recreation—all in the beautiful surroundings of the Green Mountains and the Lake Champlain basin of Vermont.

A special feature of the four-day conference was a series of public lectures that sought to look back over the last forty years of graduate theology and ministry and to look forward to the coming decades of the third millennium.

The president of St. Michael's College, Dr. Mark vanderHeyden, opened the conference by challenging theologians to engage in serious dialogue with the secular sciences lest they end up simply talking to themselves. Dermot A. Lane, in the keynote address, called for closer attention to the foundational roles of anthropology, imagination, and memory in the performance of Christian theology. Alice Laffey presented a paper on past and present developments in biblical scholarship with a keen eye on context and the future. Ray Collins highlighted the ecumenical progress that has taken place in the last forty years in the study of New Testament, especially in the complex area of different methodologies. Michael J. Fahey reviewed trends in systematic theology since 1965, paying particular attention to ecclesiology, the Trinity and Christology, and the Eucharist. Philip S. Keane summarized many of the accomplishments and new challenges facing moral theology in the future. Kevin W. Irwin outlined the christocentric character of liturgical and sacramental theology during the last forty years. Concluding reflections on the emerging issues were offered by Monika K. Hellwig, Terrence W. Tilley, and Dermot A. Lane.

Recurring themes throughout the conference were a deep concern about the ecological future of the planet, the welcome involvement of laity in the teaching of theology, the significant contribution that women are now making to theology, unresolved issues within lay ecclesial ministry in parish life, the growing gap between academic theology and pastoral practice, and the increasing importance of interreligious dialogue for Christians in the future.

The planning and organization of Reunion 2000 was undertaken by Dr. Edward Mahoney, current director of graduate theology and pastoral ministry. Much credit is due to Edward for the outstanding success of Reunion 2000. His keen attention to invitations, hospitality, travel arrangements, accommodation, liturgy, and theological renewal made the conference a rewarding experience for all. On behalf of the participants who were present at these four days in St. Michael's College in July 2000, I would like to express thanks to Edward for facilitating such a rich encounter among the participants and providing such a memorable experience.

This introduction to a publication celebrating forty years of graduate theology and pastoral ministry in St. Michael's College would be incomplete without reference to Rev. Dr. Paul Couture, SSE, and Betty Rafoul. Paul was one of the founding figures who set up the program in the early 1960s. More significant, Paul developed the summer school into one of the most successful programs in the United States throughout the '70s, '80s, and early '90s. It was Paul Couture who gave the summer program its unique character of an international faculty; high academic and pastoral standards among participants; and a strong emphasis on a vibrant community of learning, relaxation, and liturgical celebration. The hallmarks of the St. Michael's College summer program under the leadership of Paul Couture were study, prayer, and recreation.

Paul Couture was ably assisted by Betty Rafoul, a 1977 graduate of the program. Betty, in addition to acting as administrative assistant to the program, took a personal interest in promoting the well-being of students and faculty alike. Warm tributes were paid to Betty Rafoul and Paul Couture during the Reunion.

—DERMOT A. LANE

OPENING
REFLECTIONS

1. Theology in Transition

Dermot A. Lane

I am convinced that the pace of social, scientific, and technological change is having an enormous effect on theology, and that while much of this impact is negative, some of it is positive. The way we will do theology in this new century will be quite different from the last century.

The focus of this opening is on fundamental theology, concentrating on the experience of the mystery of God given in revelation, remembered in tradition, and received imaginatively through the ongoing response of faith. One could just as profitably examine systematic or moral or biblical or liturgical theology. I want to concentrate on foundational issues, however, because I believe that they are more problematic and, to some extent, are the framework out of which systematic, moral, biblical, and liturgical theologies operate. Much of the good work going on in systematic theology at present is handicapped because the principles of fundamental theology are shifting and shaking.

All of theology is contextual, and one of the lessons we learned in the twentieth century was that there is no such thing as "pure" theology. Christian theology arises out of a critical interaction between traditional faith and contemporary experience, between religion and culture, between church and society. This is especially true in the area of fundamental theology, which must address questions of faith and unbelief, apathy and love, hope and despair.

In this chapter I seek to do two things. First, I offer an analysis of some of the cultural changes affecting fundamental theology. This will necessitate a discussion of what has been happening to theology in the context of modernity and how, more recently, fundamental theology finds itself caught in the struggle between modernity and emerging postmodernity. How has fundamental theology presented itself within modernity, and what are we to make of what some describe as the dark clouds of postmodernity descending upon theology today? Similarly, the reality of pluralism must be addressed from the distinct perspectives of ecumenism and interfaith dialogue.

Second, I outline some of the resources, what I call building blocks, that might be employed in addressing the theological challenges coming from the debate about modernity and postmodernity as well as the issue of pluralism. Here I address the need for a renewed anthropology, the importance of recovering memory as a resource, and the necessity for a new religious imagination in the performance of fundamental theology.

PART I:
CULTURAL CHANGES INFLUENCING THEOLOGY

It is impossible to do theology without taking account of modernity, and no sooner has theology begun to come grips with the demands of modernity than it is faced with the puzzling prospect of postmodernity. So let us begin by looking at modernity.

1. *What Has Happened to Theology in the Period of Modernity?*

Without rehearsing the history of the Enlightenment, which gave rise to the modern era, we must refer to two highly influential figures who have left an indelible mark on modern theology. The first is René Descartes (1596–1650), who, through a process of methodic doubt, sought to come up with a foundation for clear and distinct ideas. This foundation, he discovered, in his famous "*Cogito, ergo sum*" (I think, therefore I am). This starting point, established by Descartes, issued in the turn to the subject which is one of the outstanding features of modernity.

Along with Descartes there is Immanuel Kant (1724–1804), who asked "What is the Enlightenment?" His answer was "*Sapere aude,*" which roughly translated means to have the courage to use our own reason without recourse to tradition, authority, or religion. With this response was born Enlightenment rationalism. In his application of reason alone to life, Kant made a distinction between what he called "the phenomena" of the external world, which can be known by reason, and "the noumenon," the hidden and invisible world behind the phenomena, which cannot be known by reason. This distinction has haunted theology ever since.

Descartes's "*Cogito, ergo sum*" gave rise to the emergence of the substantial, self-sufficient, sovereign subject of modernity. Kant's "*Sapere aude*" produced an emphasis on the autonomy of reason that issued in a cold, clinical, and detached rationalism. These two streams of philosophy are largely responsible for the philosophical construction of the modern world with its focus on subjective individualism and scientific, exploitative rationalism. This culture of modernity was the context in which theology sought to find its voice.

2. *The Collapse of the Classical Synthesis of God, the Cosmos, and the Self*

By far the most serious outcome of the influence of modernity upon theology has been the collapse of the ancient and premodern synthesis of God, the cosmos, and the self. As moderns we have privatized religion and God; we have stripped the cosmos of divine presence and disenchanted it; we have individualized the human self and placed it at the center of the earth. The consequences for theology have been far-reaching. The modern world has given us a natureless view of God and a godless view of nature. The universe has been mechanized and thereby stripped of all traces of transcendence. Nature has been made to serve the needs of humanity.

One of the most troubling expressions of this collapse of the relationship among God, the cosmos, and the human can to be found in the ecological crisis. Another expression of this collapse is the extraordinary degree of human estrangement, loneliness, and isolation that exists between the self and the cosmos. A further expression of this collapse can be seen in the radical secularism that permeates the whole of life, so that if there is a God, that God is no longer present to or mediated by the universe, history, or human experience. A final expression of this collapse is the separation that persists within much modern theology between nature and grace, in spite of the gallant efforts made by *la nouvelle théologie* to reunite the natural and the supernatural.

For the moment, however, I want to concentrate on what happened to our understanding of God within this culture of modernity. Many today would argue that Enlightenment rationality, namely *logos,* scientific reason, has taken over theology at the expense of *theos,* the mystery of God. There has been too much *logos* and too little *theos.* The *logos* in question, the form of rationality operating within modernity, was a rationalism devoid of affectivity, shorn of memory, and committed to the totalism of a single paradigm. Human affectivity was put aside in the name of objectivity because it could not be controlled or measured. Human memory did not count because tradition and history were suspect and the particular was subordinated to the dominance of universal reason. In its pursuit of rationalism, modernity sought a single paradigm, a scientific and universal paradigm, to which all other disciplines, including theology, had to conform. The role and function of God was merely to provide an absolute point of reference or an ultimate foundation for the claims of reason. Thereafter the mystery of God was a purely private and personal matter.

Within this admittedly oversimplified picture of modernity, two very significant things were happening in relation to theology that today are clearer in retrospect than they were in the historical unfolding of modernity. Philosophy, more especially a particular form of rationalism, was using God as a means to ground its own brand of intelligibility. Theology, in turn, if it was to have any credibility, had to conform to the canons of empirical scientific rationality to the neglect of the historical revelation of God in the Bible. Philosophy, which in previous times had been described as the handmaid of theology, was increasingly subjected to the norms of the scientific method and was now becoming the ruler of theology.

A second development within modernity was that God, the mystery of God, was being used as an item of information, a rational explanation to ground the intelligibility of the world of modern philosophy and science. In consequence, the reality of God was objectified into the category of a being among other beings. The net result of these two unfolding influences was the development of what is now called *ontotheology.*

3. The Rise of Onto-theology

The meaning of this strange-sounding term, *onto-theology*, is "the bringing together or conflation of the philosophical notion of being and the self-revelation of God of the Bible."[1] The God of the philosophers takes over the God of revelation in a way that identifies God with being, the eternal, immutable, impossible being of philosophy. This God, this absolute being of human reason, is invoked in "the service of the human project of mastering the whole of reality."[2] The God of onto-theology is ultimately a being, a super being, existing alongside other beings and therefore runs the risk of producing a form of idolatry.

A number of difficulties arise with this philosophical God of onto-theology. The first and most serious issue is the separation between the God of philosophy and the God of revelation, a separation forced upon modernity by Enlightenment's desire to be rid of tradition and authority.

A second difficulty is that onto-theology reduces God to the level of one more item and one more explanation among other items and explanations in the world. The effect of this reduction is the inevitable loss of interest in the mystery of God, which helps us to understand the stinging observation often made in the postmodern world that "God is missing but not missed."[3]

A third difficulty with onto-theology is that it implies that the highest form of knowledge is theoretical reason, a rationality that seeks control by mastering reality, especially nature. In contrast, it must be countered that Christianity is not simply about knowing the truth but primarily about doing the truth in love, a lesson we have begun to rediscover from liberation theology. In other words, Christianity is a practical way of being in the world and its credibility is to be judged not only by appeal to rational norms but also by its capacity to engender a liberating praxis in the world.

A fourth difficulty with onto-theology is the nature and character of the God it delivers. According to Heidegger it is a God before whom the individual "can neither pray nor sacrifice . . . can neither fall to his knees in awe nor can he play music and dance."[4] In spite of this insightful criticism, Heidegger's own attempt to find "the truly divine God" through the help of poets failed because it remained too much in the grip of being and did not take sufficient account of the God of the Bible.

A fifth difficulty with onto-theology is that the language used to describe God is a language of conceptual clarity and scientific objectivism—thus eliminating any sense of the limits that attach to human language in its discourse about the divine. In effect, univocal language replaces the analogical imagination of classical theology and ignores the Jewish prohibition against images of Yahweh. A complete separation of the God of philosophy from the God of Abraham, of Sarah, and of Jesus has taken place during the period of modernity with unhappy consequences for Christian theology: a theism untouched by Christology, a deism removed from the action of God in history, and a fideism blind to human mediations of the divine. Thus the transcendence of God has been domesticated by philosophy and the immanence of God controlled by reason alone.

In response to modernity Christian theology must make clear that the God of the prophets in Judaism is not the God of the philosophers, that the God of Jesus in Christianity is not the God of detached reason, and that the God of the Christian tradition is not the God of metaphysics.

Of course, it would be wrong, indeed it would be a serious misrepresentation, to suggest that Christian theology adopted *in toto* this vision of modernity. To the contrary, we know that Catholic theology right up to Vatican II shunned modernity and rejected most of its suppositions. Nonetheless, the spirit of modernity did affect and influence the shape of fundamental theology. Consider, for example, the importance given to the "proofs" for the existence of God, the focus on natural theology, and the emphasis placed on the preambles of faith within fundamental theology. In spite of attempts to ignore the Enlightenment, the spirit of modernity did infiltrate the method and content of fundamental theology, and indeed some would suggest that certain pronouncements of the magisterium did not escape the rationalistic influences of modernity.

In making this criticism of modernity and the kind of theology it generated, I do not wish to suggest that nothing of value has emerged in theology since the Enlightenment. There have been significant gains that cannot be abandoned, including the elimination of superstition from religion, the vindication of human rights for all, the cultivation of religious liberty, and the importance of justice for every human being.

Instead, what I am suggesting is that the influence of modernity upon theology, especially fundamental theology, is deeply ambiguous.

In this essay I focus more on the negative impact of modernity upon theology for two reasons. First, as we move into the twenty-first century, it has to be admitted that theology is struggling to survive within the academy for a variety of reasons—one of which is the pervasive influence of modernity. Second, the negative aspects of modernity are the background against which we can best understand the phenomenon of postmodernity.

4. A Peep at Postmodernity

I know some suggest that postmodernity is a passing fashion, one more sideshow distracting theology from the task at hand. While this reaction may have some truth to it, it nonetheless ignores the cultural vacuum that presently exists in the struggle between modernity and postmodernity, as well as the possibility that there may be fragments of truth in some of the criticisms of modernity by postmodernity.

Postmodernity, it must be noted, is more a mood than a movement, more a reaction to modernity than a worked-out philosophy, more an expression of dissatisfaction with what has been than an alternative for the future. Yet, like any reaction, it has an implicit direction.

Part of the postmodern manifesto can be summed up in the words of Jean François Lyotard: "Let us make war on totality" and "activate difference," let us acknowledge incommensurability, advance multiplicity, and promote dissensus.[5] As a reaction to modernity, postmodernity is driven by a radical deconstruction of everything informed by the Enlightenment: the deconstruction of the self, history, meta-narratives, universal reason, and God. The postmodern deconstruction of the human subject of modernity is particularly fierce and is summed up rather graphically in the words of Michel Foucault, who holds that "man is an invention of recent date" and will be "erased like a face drawn in the sand at the edge of the sea."[6] For some postmoderns the self is merely a rhetorical flourish, a linguistic and cultural device, to facilitate the interaction of differences. For others, the self is at best a site in and around which speech, transactions of power, and mechanisms of desire play themselves out[7]—a site that in effect has no unified ground or enduring field of identity. Richard Rorty sums up the position of many postmoderns when he says of the self: "There is nothing deep down inside except what we have put there ourselves."[8]

I focus here on the self of postmodernity because once the human subject is dissolved, then it follows that everything else disintegrates: history is dismantled into disconnected bits, culture is broken down into scattered fragments, meta-narratives are reduced to unrelated events, and reality is emptied of all reference. This bleak account of postmodernity prompts the question: Is there anything of value within the postmodern condition, anything worth salvaging, anything that we can learn? For many, the answer is no. Radical deconstruction leads to nihilism.

For others, there is a faint flicker of light in the darkness of postmodernity. At the center of postmodern thinking there is a strong awareness of "otherness," the other that was all too frequently forgotten, marginalized, or repressed within the narratives of Western civilization. A second feature of postmodernity attracting attention is the emphasis placed on what we do not know, a reminder of how little we do know, which resonates with the negative, *apophatic* theology of classical Christianity. A third feature among some postmodernists is a concern about the future, about the possibility of justice, about a quasi-messianic expectation or coming of what is impossible, unforeseeable, and unrepresentable.[9] There is, at least, a trace of hope implicit in the radical critiques of postmodernity.

Over and above these flickers of light within postmodernity, it has to be acknowledged that a lot of deconstructive European postmodernity as presently expressed is an unlikely alternative to modernity. The core of Christianity is circumscribed by a particular meta-narrative that embraces the close relationship that exists within the story of creation, redemption, and consummation; it is this unified story that grounds Christian faith, praxis, and worship. The Christian story is more than a construction that can be dismantled at will and whim; it is an existential reality rooted in the ongoing action of God in creation, in history, in Jesus as the Christ, and in the ecclesial community of his disciples. This does not mean that Christian faith can take for granted the credibility and coherence of this story; to the contrary, Christian faith must continually struggle to articulate the historical cogency of this meta-narrative in a way that is faithful to the Bible, tradition, and experience.

What is important about the debate between modernity and post-modernity is that it highlights the presence of a vacuum existing between the deep ambiguities of modernity and the emptiness of much of postmodernity. This, it seems to me, is the primary context in which fundamental theology must reform, renew, and transform itself in the twenty-first century. The task facing theology, therefore, is one that requires not a return to premodern forms of faith or an innocent embrace of postmodernity; instead, it necessitates a rescuing of modernity in the light of some of the critiques coming from postmodernity. In brief, there is no way of escaping the crucible of modernity within the renewal of theology.

5. Pluralism and Its Impact on Ecumenism and Interreligious Dialogue

There is a second context challenging Christian theology at the beginning of the new millennium, and that is the existence of so much pluralism: theological pluralism within the unity of Christian faith and religious pluralism among the faiths of the world. Within Christianity there is a theological pluralism inside the different confessional and denominational identities, a pluralism that goes back to the diversity of New Testament expressions of Jesus as the Christ who is the Son of God and the Word made flesh. The failure of the ecumenical movement in the latter half of the twentieth century was a failure to cope with plural-ism—both within existing denominations and across the ecclesial divides. The quest for unity by the Catholic Church or the Anglican Church with other churches that ignores the pluralism among Catholics or Anglicans themselves is as misleading as it is dishonest. The search for ecumenical unity among churches must begin to recognize that such unity can exist only within pluralism, as is the case, for example, in the gospel portraits of the Christ-event. Such pluralism can be a gift enrich-ing the depth of faith, a source of complementarity rather than conflict, and a support rather a threat.

What is perhaps even more fascinating about the ecumenical movement is that there is a new pressure on ecumenism now coming from outside the churches themselves, namely, the need for a united Christian voice within the dialogue among the other religions of the world. This new demand may in an unexpected way become one of the most effective catalysts hastening Christian unity within the diversity among the Christian churches.

Over and above the task of ecumenism there is also the challenge of interfaith dialogue. To be Christian in the future will necessitate being interreligious. This question must now be faced not only in the light of teaching of Vatican II on the other religions and the prophetic act of John Paul II at Assisi in 1986, but also in view of the new global culture. This does not mean that we have to "water down" the distinctiveness of Christian faith, or that we have to enter the discussion on a "level playing field," as some urge. If the latter were to happen, there would no real dialogue or engagement.

What are we to make of the existence of so much religious pluralism in the world today? Is it possible that such pluralism is in fact a part of God's plan of salvation for humanity? Is it conceivable that God is present and salvifically active in other religions of the world? Can we talk about the revelation of God in other religions? These questions are pressing in upon Christian consciousness in a radically new and global way as never before at the beginning of this new millennium; these are questions that will not go away and therefore must become intrinsic to the way we do fundamental theology in the future. It is against the background of this threefold context—the debate between modernity and postmodernity, the ecumenical movement, and interreligious dialogue—that I turn to the second part of this chapter. How will theology address these issues in this new century? Where will the emphasis fall? What resources are available to theology to engage these and other questions in the new millennium?

PART II:
BUILDING BLOCKS OF THE FUTURE

In seeking to respond to these questions and to address this threefold context I want to discuss the possibility of a renewed anthropology, the recovery of memory, and the importance of imagination. These three building blocks are in fact interconnected, and together, I believe, must become part of any attempt to retrieve the broken bonds among God, the cosmos, and the self within modernity. Further, I believe that these building blocks have distinctive contributions to make, as we shall see, to the urgency of ecumenism and the imperative of interreligious dialogue for theology in the twenty-first century.

1. The Renewal of Anthropology

The death of God announced by Nietzsche in the nineteenth century gave rise in the twentieth century, quite logically, to the death of the self; the death of the human subject by the deconstructive acids of postmodernity, again quite logically, is now issuing in the radical fragmentation of culture in the twenty-first century. Intimate links exist, as Karl Rahner frequently pointed out, between anthropology and theology. On the other hand, the excesses of anthropocentrism within modernity are responsible in large part for the ecological crisis of today. The import of these stark statements is that anthropology, namely, the way we understand the human, is of critical importance to our understanding of God and the cosmos.

It is hardly an exaggeration to state that the modern self is in crisis and therefore in need of reconfiguration. Evidence for this crisis is apparent from critical impulses coming from disciplines as diverse as feminism, psychology, ecology, and cosmology. As a result of this crisis, the human self is subject to constant abuse and disfigurement in public and private life.[10] Many attribute this crisis to Descartes's "*Cogito, ergo sum,*" because he more than most was responsible for the promotion of the self-sufficient, detached subject of modernity. In spite of impressive efforts to move from individualism to relationalism, some suggest this may be simply the replacement of one extreme and one stereotype by another extreme and stereotype. A more radical restructuring is required if we are, for example, to reconnect God, the cosmos, and the self.

It is now suggested by commentators like Paul Ricoeur and others that we need to move from the modern question, What is the self?, to the question, Who is the self? Descartes, in asking What is the self? was searching for a universal essence or nature of the human subject. Descartes, in answering the "what" question posited a thinking substance, which has shaped much modern anthropology. In contrast the "who" question is a search for a particular, historical agent. There is a shift in perspective between these two questions, a movement from the abstract to the concrete, from the universal to the particular, from substance to agency.[11]

The "who" question changes the focus of anthropology and concentrates on the "I" of human discourse, action, response, and transcendence. The "who" question sets out in search, not of a thing, not of pre-given reality, not of a ghost in a machine, but rather of some form of personal performance and achievement within history. The self comes into partial view by examining human discourse, by examining the "I" of human language, actions, community, and transcendence. The self begins to emerge within a narrative drawn together around discourse, action, community, and transcendence. The self is a "*homo narrans*": a subject who tells stories and an agent who acts in history. In other words, the human subject is a storied self and an active agent who is continually in process of becoming and is available through the mediation of narrative, and not, as Descartes thought, through introspection.

It is within the narrative of the storied self that human identity emerges, an identity made up of a dialectic between the underlying sameness of the self and the ongoing development of the self that Ricoeur calls "selfhood." There is a sense in which the self endures and remains the same throughout time, but there is also a sense in which the self grows and develops in the journey of life. It is this latter journey that accounts for the historical constitution of selfhood. Human identity is made up of an amalgam of the enduring sameness of the self and the historical evolution of selfhood. This relation between the sameness of self and the developing selfhood helps us to realize that the self is never quite as settled or as fixed as we might like to think, but rather contains within itself a significant degree of flexibility.[12] Think, for example, of what can happen to selfhood for better or for worse as a result of the actions associated with a career change, a new relationship, or the death of a loved one.

An even more important dialectic within the development of human identity is the relationship that exists between self and others. It is the interplay between the self and others that is primary in the constitution of human identity. This relationship between the self and others enables us to realize that the ground of the self lies outside the self, that the self comes into being through the actions of others, and that ultimately, therefore, the self is derivative, being derived from the love of others and the absolute Other we call God.

Within this interplay between the self and "the other" we begin to discover that to exist is always to coexist with others, to be is to be in relationship with others, and to develop is to be dialogical. Consequently, before one can say "I am," one must acknowledge that "we are"; prior to saying "I act," one must acknowledge that "we interact"; and in advance of proclaiming "I exist," one must acknowledge that "we belong." In the closely knit cultures of Africa, Descartes's "*Cogito, ergo sum*" is turned upside down in the claim that "we are, therefore I am" or again to invoke another instructive African saying "a person is a person through other persons."

And yet even within this shift from the "what" question to the "who" question and from the self-sufficient subject to the primacy of otherness, there is still a missing dimension: the link between the self and the cosmos. We now know in the light of the new cosmic stories coming from science that the human self is bound up in a long and complicated history going back some fifteen billion years, that we live in a finely tuned universe, and that the bonds of cosmic and chemical forces over vast periods of time have been in favor of the emergence of the human self. So strong is this support for the self that scientists now tell us that the self is made up of the ashes of dead stars,[13] that the human self is the earth in a state of self-conscious freedom, that the self bears within itself the universe just as the universe bears the self within its being.[14]

Only when this link between the self and the cosmos is rediscovered can we begin to see and retrieve the classical synthesis of God, the cosmos, and the self. Further, only when this unity between the self and the cosmos is rediscovered can we begin to look forward toward a new ethical responsibility for the care of the earth. In this way we can begin to move beyond the separation of God, the cosmos, and the self that took place in modernity and beyond the threatened dissolution of the self within the culture of postmodernity.

2. The Recovery of Memory

The second building block required in retrieving the synthesis among God, the cosmos, and the self is memory. The neglect of memory is one of the most outstanding features of the culture of modernity. As noted, one of the central aims of the Enlightenment put forward by Immanuel Kant for the promotion of a truly "objective reason" was to rid reason of the memory of the past so that humanity could face the future in complete freedom. Looking back at the Enlightenment, it is now clear there was what some call a "prejudice against memory"[15] and others refer to as a "flight from memory."[16]

The exclusion of memory from modernity has had a number of unhappy consequences. In broad terms it has produced a blinkered rationality, namely, reason shorn of memory. This neglect of memory has enabled the specifically modern myth of progress to endure throughout the last century and has helped to promote a misleading evolutionary outlook within politics. Further, this fractured reason has facilitated a large-scale denial of historical sufferings and injustices in the past, especially throughout the twentieth century. But most of all, reason divorced from memory has brought about the great divide between modernity and the biblical tradition, a divide that has resulted in the breakdown of the unity among God, the cosmos, and the self. Once reason was separated from memory, then the prophetic and healing power of memory became silenced in the period of the Enlightenment.

If these losses within modernity are to be overcome, there must be a recovery of memory, especially the prophetic and disruptive power of memory as well as its healing and liberating dynamic. One of the great secular prophets of memory in the twentieth century has been Walter Benjamin, who in turn has influenced the theology of Johann B. Metz.

Benjamin, a member of the Frankfurt school of critical theory, sought to work out what can only be described as a distinctively nonmodern view of history. His thesis was that we must read history against the grain, especially against the grain of the modern myth of progress. In 1937 Benjamin argued that we need to keep history open: "The work of the past is not closed." Max Horkheimer, a colleague of Benjamin, objected that this view of history was far too idealistic, that past injustices are past and therefore cannot be undone and that "those who were slain . . . were truly slain." Benjamin replied, "The corrective for this kind of thinking lies in the reflection that history is a form of empathetic memory. What science has settled empathetic memory can modify."[17] The past, for Benjamin, is not closed or fixed but open and unfinished. History, Benjamin points out, usually has been written by the victors and not by the victims. This fact has led to the neglect of the suffering of the victims, a neglect that allows history to repeat itself. This neglect, however, can be overcome through empathy with the victims of history. The story of the suffering of the victims can be recovered through the power of memory, provided there is empathy with the suffering of the victims of history. In this way memory can effect a unity between the past and the present, between the living and the dead. For Benjamin, every great work of civilization has also been at the same time a work of barbarism. If the barbarism of history in the past is to change, if barbarism is not to continue in the present under the guise of progress, then the present must be challenged and interrupted by the power of memory. The writings of Benjamin are scattered and unfinished but sufficiently suggestive to highlight the importance of injecting the memory of the past into the present for the creation of a different future.

This recovery of the power of memory inspired by Benjamin and taken up by Metz has much to offer as critique of both modernity and postmodernity. Memory calls into question the modern myths of progress, exposing the downside of so-called growth and development. Further, memory can keep alive the suffering and injustices endured in the past in a way that can prevent their repetition in the present. Memory, while it cannot change the past as such, it can modify the meaning of the past in the present. Past events can be interpreted differently through the healing power of memory. Memory can effect a reconciliation of past injuries in the present.

It is worth noting here that the recovery of memory is gaining ground in the light of its successful use at the Truth and Reconciliation Commission in South Africa and the recently established Truth and Memory Commission in Guatemala. This recovery of memory and its potential for the reconciliation of bruised memories is becoming an important resource in the quest for unity among Christian churches and was in part the leaven animating the 1999 Catholic-Lutheran Joint Declaration on the question of justification. The purification of past historical memories is an important step on the road to Christian unity.

If this recovery of memory is to succeed fully, however, it must have recourse to the theological primacy of memory with Judaism and early Christianity. Within Judaism it is the memory of the Passover experience and God's covenant with God's people that gives life, identity, and hope to Israel. What is distinctive about memory in the Bible is that it is not simply an objective calling to mind of past events and experiences; instead, to remember is to make available in the present a past experience or event in a way that influences the behavior of those who remember; biblical memory is about the reactualization of the past in the present. "The Hebrew recollection of the past means that what is recalled becomes a present reality."[18]

It is against this Jewish background that gives prominence to the power of memory as essential to religious identity that we must understand the final will and testament of Jesus at the Last Supper: "Do this in memory of me." Within Judaism and the early christological hymns (Eph 1:9–10; Col 1:15–20, Phil 2:5ff.) there is an awareness that the activity of God in Israel and in Jesus is an activity embracing nature and history, creation and humanity, people and cosmos. The modern separation of God from the cosmos and the self can be redressed by invoking the memory of God's action in history in the past with a view to making it active and effective once again in the present.

3. The Importance of Imagination

The invocation of memory, however, is in part dependent on the imagination. A close connection exists between the act of remembering and the exercise of the imagination. It is imagination that enables us to receive the past in the mode of memory and to point toward the future in the mode of anticipation. Through the exercise of imagination we can retrieve the past in the present and at the same time move from the present into the possibility of a new future. Imagination is the source of new and alternative ways of envisioning God, self, and cosmos.

If we look at the history of philosophy, we find more warnings against the use of imagination than recommendations in its favor. At the beginning of Greek philosophy, some four hundred years before Christianity, imagination was regarded as a lowly faculty, though by the time of Augustine imagination was valued as that faculty that gave a new vision of life which at the same time was able to embrace the presence of a divine reality.[19] Similarly, at the time of the Enlightenment imagination was regarded as inferior to the higher faculty of objective reason, which it was thought was able to deliver clear and distinctive ideas.[20]

One of the great paradoxes today is that we live in a culture in which the image reigns supreme and yet the human imagination is undervalued, underdeveloped, and little appreciated.[21] Our image-laden, postmodern culture cries out for the synthesizing and integrating functions of imagination, but by giving us so many disconnected images it has thwarted our capacity to exercise imagination. One of problems with the constant flow and play of images within postmodernity is that the images do not come with instructions about how they should be read, and all too often the image is presumed to give the full picture.[22] A similar difficulty exists in relation to the postmodern obsession with information. It is ironic that we have never had so much information available before in the history of humanity and yet so little access to meaning and truth. Information without the help of imagination is in danger of being merely digital, purely punctual, and ultimately empty.

There is at present a need to overcome past suspicions about the use of the imagination in theology and to move toward the construction of a new religious imagination. If we are to do this, then we must begin to make some distinctions in relation to imagination. Broadly, we can differentiate at least three types of imagination.[23]

There is, first of all, the ordinary, everyday use of imagination, often called the *reproductive* or the *conserving imagination.* This imagination acts as a bridge between the senses and the intellect, between image and understanding, between experience and reflection. This mediating role of the imagination enables us to synthesize the multiplicity of human experiences and within that synthesis to hold together what often appear to be contrary points of view, such as the relationship that exists between the one and the many, the same and the different, the inside and the outside.[24] In this way the human imagination can bring order out of chaos and integrate parts into the larger whole. The conserving imagination is inherited from family, community, and tradition. We depend on the use of imagination all the time, and its exercise is presupposed in all knowledge and human understanding.

In addition to the reproductive imagination there is also the *creative imagination,* which enables us to see simultaneously what is and what might be. The creative imagination helps us to see the world as suggestive of something unfamiliar by making accessible that which appears to be inaccessible, by symbolizing that which is invisible, and by putting us in touch with more than that which meets the empirical eye. This is the imagination that is alive and active in the worlds of poetry, art, and science. The exercise of the creative imagination opens up new and invisible worlds of meaning, suggesting a hidden finality to the life of nature and human affairs, and rendering complete that which appears unfinished.

Third, there is the *religious* or *theological imagination,* which seeks to go beyond the limits of conceptual thought to embrace the unknown "objects" of faith, hope, and love. In making this move the religious imagination engages in a process of affirmation, negation, and refinement through the dynamism of the human spirit. This activity is often referred to as the analogical imagination of Aquinas or the dialectic imagination of the Reformers.

What is important about the religious imagination is the dynamic capacity of the human spirit to hold together affirmations and negations in a new unity of transcendent meaning. In this way the religious imagination is able to perceive the infinite within the finite, the eternal within the temporal, and the divine within the human. Within this activity there is a movement by the spirit from the particular to the universal, from the concrete to the ultimate, from the relative to the absolute, from the part to the whole. The creative imagination, and especially the religious imagination, dares to picture the "unpicturable," to represent the unrepresentable, and to know the unknowable. If the religious imagination can do this, and surely this is an important part of the role of imagination, then a significant link may be established with the postmodern love of difference, otherness, and absence. In doing this the religious imagination nourishes and sustains the life of faith, hope, and love.

What is puzzling at present is that the exercise of the creative imagination is more apparent in the world of the arts and sciences than it is in religion and revelation. And yet as we move into the twenty-first century, it is increasingly clear that theology needs a new imagination— an imagination, first of all, that will bring together God, the cosmos, and the self into a new synthesis, and second, an imagination that can appreciate pluralism as a source of enrichment. Some of the resources that might go into this new religious imagination must surely include insights from contemporary cosmologies, the growing ecological awareness of the unity between the well-being of the earth and the well-being of humans, the new dialogue between religion and science, and many of the impulses coming from feminism. What is truly remarkable at present is how the sciences like quantum theory, astrophysics, and bio-technology can employ the use of the creative imagination without apology, and how stuck theology and religion are within the reproductive imagination, influenced more often than not by the narrow rationality of modernity.

Equally urgent at present is the need to bend, stretch, and expand the Christian imagination to embrace "the other" within interreligious dialogue. Given the teaching of the Second Vatican Council on other religions and religious freedom, the time is ripe to initiate a more intense dialogue with other faiths within the template of a new religious imagination. This new religious imagination will seek to recognize, at least, the presence of God's activity, revelation, and salvation in some of the other world religions. Further, in this new imagination we will begin to see religious pluralism as a part of God's plan for humanity in the shared search for a new global ethic for the care of the earth and the well-being of humanity. Third, this new religious imagination could become a catalyst for designing a counter-cultural ethic in the service of human rights and the bringing together of people of diverse religious beliefs in prayer and celebration linked to work of justice.

CONCLUSION

And so, to gather up these reflections, it my thesis that theology today is faced with a series of new challenges. These new challenges take us beyond the demands of the Second Vatican Council, which inspired so much of St. Michael's College summer graduate program over the last forty years. I believe that this Reunion 2000 has put down markers for future graduate programs. These markers must include reference to current debates about the viability of fundamental theology within the context of the struggle between modernity and postmodernity and the need to transform onto-theology, to face the reality of theological pluralism among and within the Christian denominations, and to engage through dialogue the presence of so much religious pluralism in the world. I believe that an important step toward addressing these challenges can be made by designing a new anthropology, by recovering the power of memory, and by invoking a new religious imagination.

NOTES

1. Michael Scanlon, "Post-modernism and Theology," *New Theology Review* (February 2000), 70.

2. Ibid.

3. The original remark is attributed to Spanish theologian Josep Vives, "Dios en el crepúsculo del signo XX," *Razón y Fe* (May 1991), 468.

4. Martin Heidegger, *Identity and Difference* (New York: Harper & Row, 1969), 70–71.

5. J. F. Lyotard, *The Post-modern Condition: A Report on Knowledge* (Manchester: Manchester University Press,1986), xxv, 82.

6. Michel Foucault, *The Order of Things: An Archeology of the Human Sciences* (New York: Random House, 1970), 387.

7. Rowan Williams, *Lost Icons: Reflections on Cultural Bereavement* (Edinburgh: T. and T. Clarke, 2000), 166.

8. Richard Rorty, *Consequences of Pragmatism* (Minneapolis, Minn.: University of Minnesota Press, 1982), xlii.

9. John D. Caputo, "Apostles of the Impossible: On God and the Gift in Derrida and Marion," in *God, the Gift and Postmodernism,* ed. John D. Caputo and Michael J. Scanlon, 197–203 (Bloomington and Indianapolis: Indiana University Press, 1999).

10. S. Rudman, *Concern for the Person in Christian Ethics* (Cambridge: Cambridge University Press, 1997), 18.

11. See Calvin O. Schrag, *The Self After Post-Modernity* (New Haven, Conn.: Yale University Press, 1999), 120.

12. Paul Ricoeur, "The Question of Selfhood," *Oneself as Another* (Chicago: University of Chicago Press, 1992), 1–25.

13. John Polkinghorne, *One World: The Interaction of Science and Theology* (London: S.P.C.K., 1986), 56.

14. Thomas Berry, *The Dream of the Earth* (San Francisco: Sierra Club Books, 1988), 132.

15. J. B. Metz, *A Passion for God: The Mystical-Political Dimension of Christianity* (New York: Paulist Press, 1998), 142.

16. Vera Schwarcz, *Bridge Across Broken Time: Chinese and Jewish Cultural Memory* (New Haven, Conn.: Yale University Press, 1998), 24.

17. References for this exchange between Benjamin and M. Horkheimer are available in Helmut Peukert, *Science Action and Foundational Theology: Towards a Theology of Communicative Action* (Cambridge, Mass.: M.I.T. Press, 1984), 206–10.

18. "Memorial, Memory," *The Interpreter's Bible* (1962/1986), 3:344.

19. G. Watson, "The Imagination and Religion in Classical Thought," in *Religious Imagination,* ed. J. P. Mackey (Edinburgh: Edinburgh University, 1986), 29.

20. R. Villadeseau, *Theological Aesthetics: God in Imagination, Beauty and Art* (Oxford: Oxford University Press, 1999), 6; see also P. Avis, *God and the Creative Imagination: Metaphor, Symbol, and Myth in Religion and Theology* (London: Routledge, 1999), 14–22.

21. Richard Kearney, *The Wake of the Imagination* (London: Hutchison, 1983), 3.

22. M. Harris, *Proclaim the Jubilee: A Spirituality for the Twenty-First Century* (Louisville, Ky.: Westminster/John Knox Press, 1996), 13.

23. I am indebted to James P. Mackey for this threefold classification. See James P. Mackey, "Theology, Science, and the Imagination: Exploring the Issues," *The Irish Theological Quarterly* 1 and 2 (1986), 1–18.

24. J. Bednar, "The Contours of the Valley: William F. Lynch S.J. and Theology," in *American Catholic Traditions: Resources for Renewal,* ed. Sandra Yocum Mize and William Portier, 135–41 (Maryknoll, N.Y.: Orbis Books, 1997), 137.

2. Biblical Scholarship:
Past, Present, and Future

Alice L. Laffey

I taught at St. Michael's College only during three summers, in 1989, 1990, and 1995. By 1995 Edward Mahoney had taken over the program from Paul Couture. At a dinner one evening, I told him that I was definitely getting too old to teach summer school; I was by then a full half-century old. Although I loved the students and the opportunity to teach adults, I did not like being separated from my home and my dog during the summer, and I needed the time to reflect and to re-create before beginning another new academic year.

But that's not all I said. I also said that, to my knowledge, between 1989 and 1995, the faculty had included only two women each summer, a clearly disproportionate number to the number of women students. I also believed that the typical student who had been the "bread and butter" of programs like "St. Mike's" was drying up, that there simply were—in 1995 and even more so now—fewer and fewer nuns needing to be recycled. I then suggested, I hope not arrogantly, that the content of a program like St. Michael's would also have to change if it was to remain alive and, more important, to continue to serve the church vibrantly as it had done during its then thirty-five year history.

Edward did not reply defensively; he assured me that there were few women faculty out there to invite, that many of the potential female faculty were booked years in advance, and that most were unwilling to commit six weeks of their summer to teach in such a program. In other words, the dearth of women faculty was not the program's fault, Paul's fault or Edward's fault but was a corollary to "historical reality." Edward then asked how I would change the program. The remarks here are based on the thoughts with which I answered Edward's question then that I think are still relevant, as well as thoughts I have gleaned since then, especially as these pertain to the field of biblical studies.

Let me begin by establishing a context for my remarks.

THE PAST

The year was 1960, two years before the opening of the Second Vatican Council. In the United States it was the beginning of "the sixties." At least some of us remember those years—within the context of American culture as well as Roman Catholicism. In 1960 the St. Michael's graduate theology and pastoral ministry program held its first sessions. That same year two doctors (one, John Rock, a devout Roman Catholic) developed what came to be known popularly as "the pill." According to a *New York Times News Service* article published 15 May 2000 in the *Worcester Telegram and Gazette*,

> The pill arrived at a time when abortion was illegal every-where in the United States and when growing numbers of young women were striving to liberate themselves from the social trappings of pre-marital chastity and vocational sup-pression. It took just five years for the pill to become the leading reversible contraceptive method in the United States. Since its introduction, an estimated 468 million American women have taken the pill. Today, more than 16 million American women are on the pill.

I juxtapose the introduction of the pill into American society and the beginnings of St. Michael's program not just because both were introduced in the same year, but because both have had profound effects. Some of those 468 million women who have used the pill have been Roman Catholics. Certainly in their first years of using the pill, many Roman Catholic women struggled painfully; what they experienced may rightly be called a conflict of interest. Nourishing the fullness of their marital relationship, a goal laudable to the church, led them to use the pill, but using the pill was a practice rejected by the church in *Humanae vitae*. Their coming to a decision in conscience to act deliberately contrary, as they understood it, to the church's teaching contributed to what some describe as a crisis of authority in the church. For most Catholic women of the early 1960s, neither the social trappings of premarital chastity nor vocational suppression was the primary motivation for using the pill; rather, the motive was the perceived economic constraints of very large families. A consequence of using the pill was that Roman Catholic married women bore fewer children. Catholic families in the past forty years have "downsized"—from six or more children to two children, or at the most three.

The 1960s also held the Second Vatican Council. Not only did the hierarchical church encourage its people to "return to the sources," it provided a *Dogmatic Constitution on Divine Revelation* that showed how scripture and tradition together constitute the depository of faith. Whereas in 1909, when Rome had established the Pontifical Biblical Commission and the Pontifical Biblical Institute to protect against the use of modern methods in the interpretation of the Bible, and whereas in 1943, when the pope had promulgated the encyclical *Divino afflante Spiritu* to allow for the guarded use of modern methods of biblical interpretation, Vatican II's decree welcomed and encouraged bible study by the laity, all those whom sex and/or calling prevent from being ordained.

At the end of the 1960s, in 1969, I, then a Sister of Mercy but technically part of the laity, entered a Presbyterian seminary to study and to be trained to teach scripture. I was a product of Vatican II and the ecumenical spirit that accompanied it. To learn to teach the Bible, I would do well to immerse myself in Protestant biblical interpretation, not because it was superior to Catholic biblical interpretation but because there had been very little Catholic interpretation of scripture in the roughly four hundred years since the Council of Trent.

The method of interpretation that predominated in that seminary as elsewhere is referred to by the umbrella term *historical criticism.* Historical criticism seeks to discover the authors who produced the biblical texts (source criticism) and the intentions of those authors; the ancient settings in which the texts originated (form criticism); and the processes by which and the purposes for which texts were combined and edited until they reached their final form (redaction criticism).

These methods of historical criticism had, since the late nineteenth century, achieved a monopoly on the goals and methods of interpreting the Bible that probably rivals the monopoly developed by Bill

Gates. The contributions of both are obvious. But just as a Florida judge has ruled against the legitimacy of Microsoft's monopoly, so also the monopoly of historical criticism was soon to be challenged and to change.

Meanwhile, Catholic students of the Bible looked to Protestant biblical scholarship and discovered centuries of well-honed historical criticism. This they rapidly devoured; they themselves also learned the skills to do historical criticism. The 1970s found Roman Catholic biblical scholars fully invested in the modern methods of biblical interpretation. This is what the teacher taught; this is what the student learned; this is what the scholar researched and produced as fruit. The effort was almost exclusively, if not totally exclusively, historical. A quick glance at the programs of the Catholic Biblical Association's annual meetings in the years since its founding in 1954 confirms my point.

In the United States today, to my knowledge, only two introductions to the Old Testament have been written by Roman Catholics, those by Lawrence Boadt and by Anthony Ceresko.[1] Larry's has an archaeological focus, which is an historical focus. Tony's has been clearly influenced by Norman Gottwald's sociological and liberationist insights but is also clearly historical in emphasis.[2] Most of the many other introductions to the Old Testament produced by Protestant biblical scholars have had a similar historical thrust.

The history of New Testament introductions is similar. Most have been written by Protestants. Both Pheme Perkins and Raymond Brown, as Catholic representatives, bring to introductory students the fruits of historical criticism.[3]

In the late twentieth century an offshoot of historical criticism emerged that is referred to as sociological criticism. Scholars who use this method apply models of society developed in the modern discipline of sociology to try to discover patterns of social construction in the ancient Near East.[4]

By the time Catholic biblical scholars had ingested historical criticism and had themselves begun to use the methodologies, some Protestant biblical scholars—Walter Wink, Brevard Childs, Walter Brueggemann, and Markus Barth, to name four—had begun to acknowledge the inadequacy of historical criticism to meet the present needs of the church faithful. Childs introduced—reintroduced, actually—canonical criticism, positing that it was not the origin of the texts and their multiple editings that was of greatest importance but the final form of the text that had been accepted as canon by the church. Instead of focusing his efforts on isolating discrete segments within a biblical book as products of different authors at different times produced for different audiences and having different purposes, Childs dared to profess that each of the biblical books should be interpreted as a whole and in light of all the other biblical books.[5] Wink, too, challenged the dominance of historical criticism, affirming—reaffirming, actually—the use of literary methods of biblical interpretation for theological ends, while Brueggemann and Barth focused their work on the theological concerns contained in the biblical texts themselves.[6] These scholars listened to the voices of faith communities dissatisfied with the assumption that the biblical texts had only one meaning, a meaning confined to the past, to be found in their authors' intentions; these scholars pressured for an *aggiornamento*, a methodological "opening of the windows."

Ricoeur's theory of interpretation and Gadamer's hermeneutics gradually gained a hearing with at least some members of the scholarly biblical community.[7] Literary criticism, including close reading, narrative criticism, structuralism, and even deconstruction began to emerge as viable methods of biblical interpretation.[8] These methods looked to the text itself, rather than to the history that lay behind the text, as the primary source of a text's meaning. They allowed for a surplus of meaning, that texts could legitimately mean something more or something different from what their original authors had intended, and, implicitly, that texts could legitimately have more than one meaning. Reader-response criticism recognized the role of the reader in the act of interpretation.

Literary criticism was soon followed by feminist and ecofeminist biblical criticism and other liberationist and postmodern approaches.[9] These focused not only on the interpreter but especially on those interpreters who had traditionally been excluded from the interpretation process—women, African-Americans, and persons from the Two-thirds World. While they used both historical and literary methodologies, they placed these at the service of the social location of the interpreter, acknowledging the vested interests of the social location of the interpreting community in the act of interpretation. Once the vested interests of interpreting communities were incorporated into the interpretative process, scholars began to recognize the presence of underlying ideological assumptions in the biblical texts themselves and to do ideological criticism. The mid-1970s through the present have seen many methods and approaches to biblical interpretation.[10]

In 1993 the Pontifical Biblical Commission published a document entitled *The Interpretation of Scripture in the Church,* that commemorated the fiftieth anniversary of the encyclical that had first allowed Roman Catholics to uses modern methods of biblical interpretation: *Divino afflante Spiritu. The Interpretation of Scripture in the Church* reviewed all the methods of biblical interpretation that were at scholars' disposal in 1993—those cited above—and commented on the value and limitations of each. The document posits the eventual benefits of the methods for the ecclesial community as the criterion by which to measure each method's value.

This material bridges the past with the present.

THE PRESENT

In the forty years since the introduction of the pill into American society and the introduction of St. Michael's program in graduate theology and pastoral ministry, much has changed—in society as well as in the church. Thanks to Dr. Rock and associates, most American families have fewer members; both parents work and the family experiences, generally speaking, greater affluence; many children are described as "latch-key kids" and are recipients of very expensive day care. The society has experienced a second wave of feminism and the legalization of abortion; Americans have experienced the Vietnam War. Nixon's resignation and Clinton's impeachment have combined to diminish national confidence in political leadership.

As church, we also have experienced radical changes. Catholic biblical scholars have made strong contributions to biblical scholarship in historical criticism and in the alternative methodologies that have developed since 1960. The implementation efforts after Vatican II have helped to shape our consciousness of ourselves as "the people of God" and have contributed both to making us more active and responsible laity within the church and to relativizing for us the importance of the church's hierarchical structure and the magisterium. Moreover, well-publicized incidents of sexual misconduct and financial mismanagement have served to diminish our confidence in traditional church leadership.

Sandra Schneiders sets forth the believing community, not the church's magisterial authority, as the authentic and privileged interpreter of scripture.[11]

Forty years after Vatican II ecumenism has made great progress. The Roman Catholic–Anglican dialogue and the Catholic–Lutheran dialogue have each drafted working papers toward Christian unity. Bryan Hehir, a Roman Catholic priest, became dean at Harvard's Divinity School where (as at Yale) Roman Catholic women comprise the largest single denomination of students. Roman Catholic faculty in the Department of Religious Studies at Holy Cross, as one example, hold doctoral degrees from Yale, Temple, Vanderbilt, Harvard, and the University of Chicago, as well as from the Jesuit School of Theology at the University of California at Berkeley, the University of Notre Dame, and the Biblicum. Not only is biblical scholarship essentially ecumenical, many—biblical people and others—have shifted to (or developed) a self-understanding that is primarily Christian and only secondarily Roman Catholic. They recognize that the Christian Bible belongs to Christianity in all its ecclesial expressions.

Enter *Ex corde ecclesiae*. The Vatican, because of its concern for the education of Catholics in their tradition—the ecclesial expression of Christianity that gave birth to the St. Michael's program—is seeking to safeguard the orthodox handing on of doctrine in Catholic colleges and universities throughout the world. To shore up the schools' Catholic identity it is trying to ensure (1) that a majority of each school's trustees is Catholic; (2) that a majority of each school's faculty is Catholic; (3) that, if at all possible, each school's president is Catholic, and (4) that all teachers of Catholic theology receive a *mandatum* to teach from the local bishop. This last provision is an attempt to make sure that what Catholic theologians are teaching is authentically Catholic.[12]

Let me first try to provide, if not an explanation exactly, a context for this seemingly less than ecumenical posture. James Davidson, a Catholic sociologist from Purdue University who teaches at the University of Indiana at Indianapolis, has used the category of *generations*— rather than the usual sociological categories of gender, race, and class—to distinguish different types of American Catholics.[13] He contends that people are born into a specific social context and that experiences that take place during the formative years—between ages 11 and 21—have a defining effect and leave a lasting impression on their lives.

Davidson distinguishes among four Roman Catholic generations: (1) pre–Vatican II types, those born before 1940, who are now 60 years old or older; (2) Vatican II Catholics, those born between 1940 and 1960, who are now between 40 and 60 years of age; (3) the post–Vatican II generation, those born between 1961 and 1980, who are now approximately between the ages of 20 and 40; and (4) those born after 1980.

Davidson's research has established five characteristics of American Catholics that are shared by all these generations:

1. Belief in a need for greater democratic decision-making in the church. Davidson accounts for this by what he calls the "American cultural consensus," conforming to American values, including the importance given in our culture to the individual and his or her personal growth;
2. A belief in the core doctrines of the church—the Trinity, the Incarnation, the Resurrection, Mary, the real presence.
3. Influenced by the church's social teachings, Catholics are concerned about other people and believe they have a duty to help close the gap between the rich and the poor;
4. A belief in the importance of the sacraments—the need to have priests to visit the sick, and so forth—and thus a willingness to ordain married men and to have men who had been priests and then married serve as priests;
5. Adoption of new devotional practices such as bible study and prayer groups.

However, and even more important as a context for *Ex corde ecclesiae*, Davidson's research has also distinguished differences among the generations:

1. *Mass Attendance:* While fewer than one-third of American Catholics across the generations attend Mass regularly, fewer than one-fifth of the post–Vatican II generation of American Catholics do.
2. *Marriage:* More members of the post–Vatican II generation of American Catholics (40%) marry non-Catholics than did Catholics of either the pre–Vatican II or Vatican II generations,[14] more than half of the marriages between a Catholic and a non-Catholic take place outside the church.

3. *Devotional Practices:* There has been a considerable decrease in prayers and practices such as the rosary, the stations of the cross, Benediction of the Blessed Sacrament, and so forth; only about one-fourth of the post–Vatican II generation of American Catholics finds such practices meaningful.
4. *Institutional Church:* The post–Vatican II generation and many of those born soon after 1980[15] are less committed to the institutional church and place less confidence in its teaching authority; they are more open to artificial means of birth control, divorce and re-marriage, abortion, and the ordination of women.
5. *Catholic Identity:* The post–Vatican II generation of Catholics is less likely to say that it is important to be Catholics and less likely to raise its children Catholic.
6. *Individual Decision-making:* The post–Vatican II generation of American Catholics and many of those born soon after 1980 believe that it is the individual's right to make decisions about birth control, sex outside marriage, homosexuality, and so on.

Catholic sociologist Patricia Wittberg, a woman religious who teaches at the University of Indiana at Indianapolis, complements Davidson's findings with gender statistics that suggest that there are more practicing post–Vatican II men than there are women.[16]

Davidson, using Wittberg's data as well as his own, warns that the scenario—Catholics raised Catholic in Catholic homes, then falling away from the practice of their faith in adolescence or early adulthood, then with marriage and the beginnings of a new family returning to church participation—will no longer be the case. Since considerably fewer are being raised Catholic in Catholic homes, there will not be any-thing to return to. The scenario seems to be worse for women because the church's teachings on sexuality have been problematic.

As a corollary, the theological community itself is aging; whereas the laity of the Vatican II generation sought education in theology, very few of the post–Vatican II generation of American Catholics have pur-sued careers in theology.

Now what does all this have to do with the present in its relation-ship to the field of biblical studies? Let me briefly suggest two insights—one from the biblical texts themselves, and one from method-ological considerations. Historical scholarship has demonstrated that after Israel's return from exile, one group wished to re-create God's covenant people as a national group—and therefore was vehement in its efforts to exclude people of mixed blood, for example, the Samaritans (see Hag 2:10–14; Neh 13:3; Ezra 9:1–3) and foreign wives (see Neh 13:23–25; Ezra 10:10–12). This group also demanded absolute observance of Sabbath rest (see Neh 13:19–22).

But what of the people who had become somewhat culturally assimilated while they were in exile? Should these not be included as part of Israel's covenant people? The Book of Ruth answers a resounding yes. Ruth, a Moabite, from the despicable people of Moab (cf. Deut 23:3–4; 2 Kgs 1:1) is good enough to become the ancestor of the great king David; faithfulness to God, therefore, not national identity, should be the determinant of the legitimacy of one's inclusion in the covenant community. The narrative of the prophet Jonah also answers a resounding yes. It is not the Hebrew prophet but the despised Assyrians who hear the word of the Lord and obey; Jonah runs from the presence of the Lord while the Assyrians don sackcloth, put ashes on their heads, fast, and repent their sins.

The tension generated by the questions of belonging—Who are insiders? outsiders? Should a community include outsiders? How can a community include outsiders without ceasing to be what it is?—are not new questions, arising from new predicaments, dilemmas created by post–Vatican II ecumenism. For more than two thousand years there has been a balancing act—often in the form of a see-saw—moving between open-door and closed-door policies in the creation and maintenance of the integrity of believing communities.

Let me give another example that emerges from the use of modern methodologies (that is, historical criticism) in the interpretation of biblical texts. A historical approach identifies Gen 19:1–11—the narrative regarding two angels who visit Sodom before the city's destruction—with the importance of ancient Israelite laws of hospitality and denies that its writers had any intention of condemning homosexuality.[17] One crosses the bridge to theology, however, when one concludes that because the intention of the author of the Bible—or at least of the author of Gen 19:1–11—was not to condemn homosexual behavior to its original audience that this text provides no biblical basis for the condemnation of homosexual behavior today and, consequently, that homosexual behavior should not, based on the Bible, be condemned today.

The Pontifical Biblical Commission's document *Interpreting the Bible in the Church* suggests that biblical scholars should not do historical criticism as an end in itself but rather that they have a responsibility to the ecclesial community. *Ex corde ecclesiae* stresses, however, that theologians must teach in accord with the teaching of the church. Even as I speak, the Vermont legislature has voted to afford homosexuals who are in long-term, same-sex relationships the same legal rights to certain benefits as married people, but the sixteen New England bishops have signed a document in response to Vermont's new law that opposes it. The biblical scholar who is a historical critic affirms that the biblical texts that explicitly name homosexual behavior do not have as their primary motive, as their author's primary intention, the condemnation of homosexual behavior. The biblical scholar whose methodologies are theological, if Catholic, is supposed to, according to the norms of *Ex corde ecclesiae*, very clearly set forth the church's teaching that rejects homosexual practice. One can only ask whether and to what extent this will become another instance of conflict of interest.

THE FUTURE

Based on what we know of the past forty years and what we know in the present, can anything be said about our future? To what extent do we influence society and also the church? To what extent is the future beyond our control? Does looking ahead in the short term suggest scenarios that contrast with future long-term possibilities? What does the future hold for biblical studies, including Catholic biblical studies? What does the future hold for St. Michael's program in graduate theology and pastoral ministry?

The Future of Biblical Scholarship

1. Multiple methodologies are here to stay. Whereas Catholics entered the field of biblical scholarship when it was almost exclusively dominated by the methodologies of historical criticism, the field now embraces many methodologies, and many of these presuppose the validity of interpretation for the contemporary community. Catholic biblical scholars are very much involved.

In the short term many Catholic biblicists may be tempted to return to the protection afforded them by historical criticism and thereby avoid the danger of suggesting contemporary theological interpretations of biblical texts that are contrary to the church's official teaching. Moreover, some younger scholars may prefer the meaning of the text rather than an array of possible and legitimate meanings, convinced that multiplicity and choice diminish authority.

In the long run, though, the thrust of the biblical texts, including the New Testament injunction not to judge and the imperative "to love one another," will, I believe, continue to present doctrinal challenges and moral critiques to a theology that does not hear the lived experience of the faithful and to a church whose practice is inconsistent with its theology. The social location of the believing community demands that biblical scholars proclaim and profess the radical liberation of the gospel message as well as ecclesial responsibility.

2. There are fewer younger Catholic teachers of scripture, just as there are fewer priests and fewer nuns. Moreover, these younger teachers have been formed in a very different world from their predecessors. They live, as David Gentry has pointed out,

> not in a world of "givens," but in a world of options; the Roman Catholic tradition is just one more option. Even within Roman Catholicism, they often feel free to pick and choose, to practice a kind of eclecticism. They "create" the self by trying on different styles, different points of view, in a more or less fluid way. Because their starting point lies in personal experience, they are not preoccupied with a need for either consistency or structure.[18]

It is futile to argue against "cafeteria Catholicism"; for very many, it is the *modus operandi.*

I suggest that the contemporary forms of "cafeteria Catholicism" began with artificial birth control and the church's response in *Humanae vitae* and have spread to tubal ligations, respect for lesbians and gays involved in long-term loving relationships, divorced and remarried Catholics, and so forth. A few young American Catholics may experience the church's structure as attractive precisely because it represents a stability they have never had, and a small number of these who become bible teachers may prefer historical criticism for its (seeming) stability. By and large, however, the biblical teacher of the near future will tolerate multiple readings and interpretations of a single biblical text.

3. There are fewer students of the scriptures. Fewer Catholics are encountering the biblical texts where they first did, in the liturgy, because fewer younger Catholics are celebrating the liturgy regularly.

> Students who take religion classes today seek reasons to believe. Their levels of commitment to the very notion of religion vary. The questions that, historically, gave rise to theology—Does life have meaning? Is there a God? Who is Jesus?—are their questions.[19]

For these students the revelation of God in Jesus as glimpsed through the scriptures can be filled with meaning and life-giving.

4. The gender factor cannot be minimized. Mainstream biblical scholarship attests to the patriarchal character of the biblical texts. Some feminist biblical scholars trained in historical criticism, Jewish and Christian, have rejected the biblical texts as having nothing good to say to contemporary women; they blame the biblical texts for legitimating patriarchal practices in contemporary society and in the churches. Others claim the liberationist thrust of the texts as good news while owning the texts' patriarchal character. These scholars seek to retrieve as salvific those elements in the text that they experience as liberating and life-giving. When all is said and done, however, most feminist biblical scholars recognize that the use of established historical methods of biblical study led to the uncovering of the patriarchal biases of the texts and has contributed, along with pastoral insensitivity, to the alienation of many women from a male-dominated church.

5. Mugabe, the present president of Zimbabwe, has pointed out to the people of Africa that "when the colonizers came, the Africans had the land and the colonizers had the Bible, but that within a few short years, the colonizers had the land, and the Africans had the Bible." In the short term there have arisen African biblical scholars whose approach to

the texts has been liberationist. Whether in the long run many Africans will reject Christianity and its biblical roots as part of the propaganda of the oppressor, I don't know. What I do know, though, is that selected texts from the Bible were used, toward Africans as well as African-Americans, as a tool of oppression. Whether postcolonial cultures will walk a path similar to the women who, while acknowledging the Bible's biases, have nevertheless affirmed its essentially liberationist thrust, only time will tell.[20]

The Future of St. Michael's Program: Pastoral Ministry and Graduate Theology

As long as the students who apply to St. Michael's program were born before 1960, graduate theology and pastoral ministry can continue with its traditional curriculum. However, there are simply fewer and fewer of these students to attract. If St. Michael's wishes to attract younger students, however, enough students to maintain its program and, even more important, to continue to serve the church effectively as it has done for the past forty years, it is my contention that the program must do a couple of things.

First, it must continue its ecumenical openness. Despite *Ex corde ecclesiae*'s emphasis on "Catholic" in the narrower, Roman sense, the community of the faithful has, since Vatican II, moved in the direction of a more catholic (with a small "c"), that is, more universal sense. Because Catholics live in their culture, I see no turning back on this—even if I would wish to, which I do not.

Second, the program must conscientiously seek to attract that more than 80 percent of the baptized community who are "cafeteria Catholics"—who seem to have either dropped out or never really dropped in—as well as the less than 20 percent who "attend Mass regularly," as Davidson has characterized them. I submit that the classroom must address the wide range of human experiences of students that may propel them to the Transcendent, for example, a course that feels with the suffering, a course that walks the path to death, a course whose expressed goal is to seek ways to alleviate loneliness and alienation. These are human experiences that young people today have, and they are seeking ways to interpret these experiences. St. Michael's believes that the Christian tradition has something worthwhile to say to these people, something that transcends their experiences and that is potentially more life-affirming than society's responses—whether resignation, pain management, or any of many self-help books that society offers. The theology must be taught, however, not divorced from these human experiences but in real dialogue with them. Building community, survivors' supports, the challenges of loving in long-term, committed relationships, the ecological crisis—these human experiences and/or goals are present in human consciousness and provide opportunities to transcend human selfishness and open out to a loving God who empowers and frees the individual and society to reach beyond themselves. Led from real experiences in society, one can then ask the foundational questions: What is life's meaning? Who is God? What can gospel accounts of the life of Jesus teach us about divine revelation?

The post–Vatican II Catholics for whom graduate theology has appeared attractive (a very few from that less than 20 percent post–Vatican II church-going set) may wish the program to flow from graduate theology to pastoral ministry. Wanting first to investigate the foundational questions—life's meaning, divine revelation, and the like—they may then wish to move to how revelation and theology can comfort and liberate what is too often experienced as a self-contained world. These students will wish to explore the kerygma, the church's core teaching, assuming its value as a tool to make sense of people's experiences. A curriculum whose starting point is grounded in concrete human experiences must balance a curriculum whose theology is more speculative.

Finally, I suggest that St. Michael's program in pastoral ministry must risk traversing dangerous territory if it is to enter into meaningful conversation with—a conversation that includes respectful listening to—the difficult questions associated with living in contemporary American society, issues that affect women especially but not exclusively: the tubal ligations that are the recommended medical response to twenty or more years on the pill, domestic violence, rape, abortion, premarital sex, as well as other sexual issues such as condoms and AIDS, issues such as alcohol and other drug abuse, and the increase of violence generally in our society, its perpetrators and its victims, and capital punishment. Otherwise the program will limit its interlocutors to the naive, the inexperienced, and the saved but turn a deaf ear to the real and large percentage of its own community whose primary fault is to have been born in the United States after 1960. How many traditional families do you know? How many with divorce? With a homosexual child? With alcohol and drug problems? And the list goes on. . . .

Jesus, as portrayed in the gospels, gets to the nitty-gritty of the human experiences of the people he loves; he affirms the paralyzed, the prostitute, the leper, the tax collector, generally speaking, the marginal—and have you noticed, these are the people the religious establishment does not understand?

A FUTURE GROUNDED IN HOPE

The Christian Bible to which Roman Catholics were asked by the Second Vatican Council to return, when asked to "return to the sources" and to consider Revelation as "Scripture and Tradition," seeking the origins of the Tradition (with a capital T) in Scripture, contains truly good news. It is my hope that the future of biblical scholarship holds the proclamation of this good news.

The ancient texts were not directed to an audience of PhD's or even MA's. They were, however, directed—as we believe, by the inspiration of God and the community's leadership—toward open, intelligent, and rational communities. We have professionalized the study of the scriptures partly because the world of 1000 B.C.E. or even 100 C.E. is far different from our world today. The Bible's languages are Hebrew and Greek, not English; their culture was considerably more agrarian, though they had cities; theirs was a culturally very different world from our own. And so experts have studied the history and cultures that produced the texts—and such has been necessary. But the scriptures contain insights that while produced by and directed to a particular historical and sociological context can also be interpreted, as David Tracy would recognize (or Thomas Aquinas before him), by an analogical imagination. Let us look at how all of us, students of the biblical texts, might use an analogical imagination to internalize as well as to proclaim insights from the scriptures for the future.

The Old Testament seems to present, for the most part, a special community, one nation Israel, one chosen people in contrast to others. This community is admonished, "Take no revenge and cherish no grudge. You shall love your neighbor as yourself" (Lev 19:18). But a few verses later the Israelites are also commanded, "Love the stranger/ alien as yourself, for you were strangers/aliens in the land of Egypt" (Exod 23:9; Lev 19:34; Deut 10:19). They are to treat the alien living in their land the same way that they would wish to be treated, even including them in the Passover if they wish to be included (Exod 12:49). The Exile clearly brings with it a new understanding of Israel's relationship to the outsider.

The books of the prophets are filled with the people's responsibilities to the widow, the fatherless, and the poor—as well as to the stranger. The texts are many too many to quote, but the direction is clear: godly behavior protects the society's vulnerable, in this case, persons whom patriarchal social structures make most vulnerable (the woman who has lost her husband, the child who has lost his or her father, the family that has lost its access through the father to economic well-being) and those who otherwise do not belong. Isaiah, Micah, Leviticus are filled with covenantal stipulations to care for . . . (cf. Deut 24:19–21; 25:12–13; 27:19).

And then there is the book of Jeremiah in which Nebuchadnezzar is described as the "servant of the Lord," and Second Isaiah in which the Persian King Cyrus is designated the Lord's anointed, and the book of Ruth whose heroine is a Moabite, and the book of Jonah in which the detestable Assyrians obey the word of the Lord.

But usually Christians push aside the Old Testament when considering Jesus' love command: "This is my commandment, that you love one another as I have loved you" (Jn 15:12) and "No one has greater love than this, to lay down one's life for one's friends" (vs. 13). And the gospel of Matthew notes Jesus' affirmation of action by recording as one of his sayings, "Not everyone who says to me, 'Lord, Lord,' will enter the kingdom of heaven, but the one who does the will of my Father in heaven" (Matt 7:21).

Scrutiny of the portraits of Jesus in each of the gospels, despite the different social locations of the books' authors, and the differences in the texts, provides fragments of a portrait of Jesus as acting in inclusive and loving ways. His anger and rejection are consistent: toward those who would exclude, who would legalistically interpret the law, who would be insensitive to the physical needs of others as well as to their spiritual needs and longings (e.g., Matt 15:1–20; Lk 11:37–52; Jn 2:13–16).

What about the woman with a hemorrhage (Mk 5:25–34)? In her

social context she was ritually unclean; her motivation made no difference. She was materially, bleeding. She was, by the synagogue's rules, legitimately to be excluded. Bleeding women were unclean and certainly unable to participate in ritual. But she dared to touch Jesus—the temple of God according to John 2—and that was okay. Her daring, her arrogance, her guts, her courage, her desperation and her demand to be included were honored.

And then there's the leper—to be placed outside the camp lest he contaminate (Matt 8:1–3; Mk 1:40–42). The risk of contamination led to social ostracization. He who was physically impaired became socially impaired and economically impaired. And so it is in our society. The physically impaired—depending on their "challenge"—cannot take initiative socially and can often not support themselves economically. One thing leads to another and they become "objects"—of pity, perhaps, but objects. Jesus' relationship to the lepers was a posture of acceptance, not of rejection, a posture of healing. And in Luke's version the only leper who returned to thank him was from the despised Samaritans.

And then there's Matthew the tax collector (Matt 9:9), and Nicodemus, the Pharisee (Jn 3), and the rich tax collector Zaccheus (Lk 19:2). Jesus sat and ate with tax collectors and sinners. Moreover, he never demanded change as a condition for his outgoing posture toward institutional outsiders. Even to those to whom he is recorded as saying, "Go, and sin no more," he does not say, "If you sin no more, you can walk. . . ."

It appears that Jesus didn't have standards—at least standards that justified exclusion. "Let the little children come unto me. . . . Feed the hungry, clothe the naked. . . ." He himself is depicted as forgiving the man being crucified—for God knows what—with him.

Who was he angry with? The people who needed proof (Thomas), those who sought personal profit at a place of worship (Jn 2), those who were concerned with their own status and recognition (first places at table, even the request by the mother of Jesus' disciples that her sons might sit at Jesus' right hand), those who legalistically sought their security in details that would control others.

Then there's the Roman centurion (Matt 8:5), and the Syro-Phoenician woman (Mk 7:26). More outsiders. . . .

Who were the ones most likely to "miss the boat"? Was the judgment against the Pharisees because they were evil, or because they had

God under control, and controlled access to God (or so they thought). When do laws and customs become obstacles? It is my hope that together we can continue to proclaim this good news!

CONCLUSION

What I have tried to do is share with you my own experience. As a biblical scholar whose social location as a believing Catholic led to my graduate work in biblical studies, and whose experience as a teacher of both undergraduate 18 to 22 year olds as well as older graduate students, I have worked in a rapidly changing American technological society in which lies the American church, as part of a global church, a church that has also radically changed since 1960 and since St. Michael's first program in graduate theology and pastoral ministry. I have tried to represent the past forty years fairly, though not as comprehensively as I might have liked; I have tried to represent the present honestly, though because of its fragmentation and my own, not as cohesively as I might have liked; and I have tried to project the future for biblical studies and for St. Michael's, though not as clearly and in as much detail as I might have wished.

I am basically optimistic about the future. The self-transcending message of the gospel can only become more attractive to our broken world; although the laborers may be few, I believe that God's message through the scriptures is good news, and truly good news will always be welcome.

NOTES

1. Lawrence Boadt, *Reading the Old Testament: An Introduction* (Mahwah, N.J.: Paulist Press, 1985); Anthony R. Ceresko, *Introduction to the Old Testament: A Liberation Perspective* (Maryknoll, N.Y.: Orbis Books, 1992).

2. Norman K. Gottwald, *The Hebrew Bible: A Sociological Introduction* (Philadelphia: Fortress Press, 1985).

3. Pheme Perkins, *Reading the New Testament: An Introduction* (Mahwah, N.J.: Paulist Press, 1988); Raymond E. Brown, *An Introduction to the New Testament*, Anchor Bible Reference Library (New York: Doubleday, 1997).

4. See, for example, Bruce Malina, *The New Testament World: Insights from Cultural Anthropology* (Nashville, Tenn.: Westminster/John Knox Press, 1993); idem, *The Social World of Jesus and the Gospels* (New York: Routledge, 1996); Bruce Malina and John Pilch, eds., *Handbook of Biblical Social Values* (Peabody, Mass.: Hendrickson Publishers, 1998). See also Victor H. Matthews and Don C. Benjamin, *The Social World of Ancient Israel 1250–587 BCE* (Peabody, Mass.: Hendrickson Publishers, 1993).

5. Brevard Childs, *Introduction to the Old Testament as Scripture* (Philadelphia: Fortress Press, 1979). Cf. Paul R. Noble, *The Canonical Approach: A Critical Reconstruction of the Hermeneutics of Brevard S. Childs,* Biblical Interpretation no. 16 (Leiden: E. J. Brill, Academic Publishers, Inc. 1995).

6. Walter Wink, *The Bible in Human Transformation: Toward a New Paradigm of Biblical Study.* Cf. Wink's *Naming the Powers: The Language of Power in the New Testament,* vol. 1 (Philadelphia: Fortress Press, 1984); *The Powers That Be: Theology for a New Millennium* (New York: Doubleday and Co., 1999). Walter Brueggemann, *Hopeful Imagination: Prophetic Voices in Exile* (Philadelphia: Fortress Press, 1986); idem, *Abiding Astonishment: Psalms, Modernity and the Making of History, Literary Currents in Biblical Interpretation* (Louisville, Ky.: Westminster/John Knox Press, 1991); idem, *Finally Comes the Poet: Daring Speech for Proclamation* (Minneapolis: Fortress Press, 1989); Walter Brueggemann and George Stroup, eds., *Many Voices, One God: Being Faithful in a Pluralistic World,* in honor of Shirley Guthrie (Louisville, Ky.: Westminster/John Knox Press, 1998); Markus Barth, *Ephesians: Introduction, Translation, and Commentary on Chapters 1–3,* Anchor Bible 34 (Garden City, N.Y.: Doubleday, 1974); idem, *Ephesians: Introduction, Translation and Commentary on Chapters 4–6,* Anchor Bible 34A (Garden City, N.Y.: Doubleday, 1974); idem, *Colossians: A New Translation with Introduction and Commentary,* Anchor Bible 34AB (Garden City, N.Y.: Doubleday, 1995).

7. Paul Ricoeur, *Interpretation Theory: Discourse and the Surplus of Meaning* (Fort Worth, Tex.: Texas Christian University Press, 1976); Cf. Hans Georg Gadamer, *Truth and Method* (New York: Continuum, 1993).

8. For an example of narrative criticism, see Sharon Pace Jeansonne, *The Women of Genesis: From Sarah to Potiphar's Wife* (Minneapolis: Fortress Press, 1990). For deconstruction, see David Rutledge, *Reading Marginally: Feminism, Deconstruction and the Bible,* Biblical Interpretation Series no. 21 (New York: Brill, 1996).

9. Important examples include Phyllis Trible, *God and the Rhetoric of Sexuality* (Philadelphia: Fortress Press, 1978) and *Texts of Terror* (Philadelphia: Fortress Press, 1984); Elisabeth Schüssler Fiorenza, *In Memory of Her: A Feminist Reconstruction of Christian Origins* (New York: Crossroad, 1983) and *Bread Not Stone: The Challenge of Feminist Biblical Interpretation* (Boston:

Beacon Press, 1994). See also George Aichele, Fred W. Burnett, and Elizabeth A. Castelli, eds., *The Postmodern Bible: The Bible and Culture Collective* (New Haven, Conn.: Yale University Press, 1995); and A. K. M. Adam, *What Is Postmodern Biblical Criticism?,* Guides to Biblical Scholarship (Minneapolis: Fortress Press, 1995).

10. For African-Americans, see, for example, Cain Hope Felder, ed., *Stony the Road We Trod: African American Biblical Interpretation* (Minneapolis: Fortress Press, 1991); for the Two-thirds World, see, for example, R. S. Sugirtharajah, ed., *Voices from the Margin: Interpreting the Bible in the Third World* (Maryknoll, N.Y.: Orbis Books, 1995). See also Fernando F. Segovia and Mary Ann Tolbert, eds., *Reading from This Place: Social Location and Biblical Interpretation in the United States,* vol. 1 (Minneapolis: Fortress Press, 1995) and *Reading from This Place: Social Location and Biblical Interpretation in Global Perspective*, vol. 2 (Minneapolis: Fortress Press, 1995); David Jobling, ed., *Ideological Criticism of Biblical Texts,* Semeia 59 (Atlanta: Scholars Press, 1993); and David Penchansky, *The Betrayal of God: Ideological Conflict in Job*, Literary Currents in Biblical Interpretation (Louisville, Ky.: Westminster/John Knox Press, 1990).

11. Sandra M. Schneiders, *The Revelatory Text: Interpreting the New Testament as Sacred Scripture* (Collegeville, Minn.: Liturgical Press, 1999).

12. Soon after the American Bishops endorsed a document on how they would work to strengthen the Catholic identity of colleges in the United States, Richard McBrien of the University Notre Dame published in *America* magazine his profession of why he would not request a *mandatum* from the local ordinary. In early June 2000, at the College Theology Society meeting (the annual meeting of college teachers of theology), Bishop Leibrecht, the chair of the bishops' committee responsible for the American document on the implementation of the norms of *Ex corde ecclesiae*, urged all Catholic theologians present, in a spirit of *communio,* to seek a *mandatum.*

13. The data contained here and in the following paragraphs was presented by Dr. Davidson at the College Theology Society meeting at Villanova University, 2 June 2000. See also James D. Davidson, *The Search for Common Ground: What Unites and Divides Catholic Americans* (Huntington, Ind.: Our Sunday Visitor, 1997); James D. Davidson, William V. D'Antonio, Dean R. Hoge, and Ruth A. Wallace, eds., *American Catholic Laity in a Changing Church* (Kansas City, Mo.: Sheed and Ward, 1989), and *Laity: American and Catholic: Transforming the Church* (Kansas City, Mo.: Sheed and Ward, 1996).

14. While Davidson's differences among the generations show the greatest contrast between the post–Vatican II generation and the other generations, the differences can be found, to a lesser extent, between the pre–Vatican II and Vatican II generations.

15. Davidson's fourth Roman Catholic generation, those born after 1980, includes both the young who do what their parents do and believe what they are taught as well as adolescents and young adults. Among the latter, those whom I identify as having been born soon after 1980, are those who follow the perspective of the post–Vatican II generation and those who staunchly reject it. Yet even those who reject the attitudes and behavior of the post–Vatican II generation and seem to share attitudes and behavior more closely aligned to the pre–Vatican II generation have had a very different cultural formation that must be acknowledged.

16. The data contained here was presented by Dr. Wittberg to the members of the College Theology Society attending its annual meeting at Villanova University, 2 June 2000. See also Patricia Wittberg, *The Rise and Decline of Catholic Religious Orders: A Social Movement Perspective,* SUNY Series in Religion, Culture and Society (Albany, N.Y.: State University of New York Press, 1994) and idem, *Pathways to Re-Creating Religious Communities* (Mahwah, N.J.: Paulist Press, 1996). A questionnaire that Holy Cross gives to entering first-year students and then again to the same group as graduating seniors confirms Sister Patricia's findings. A question posed to the 1999 graduating class that asked about the student's religiosity revealed that fewer women than men considered themselves religious when entering college and fewer still—and fewer than men—considered themselves religious at graduation.

17. See Walter Wink's theological approach in *Homosexuality and Christian Faith: Questions of Conscience for the Churches* (Minneapolis: Fortress Press, 1999).

18. Private email from Dr. Gentry-Aikin, assistant professor in the department of theology, St. Mary's College, Moraga, California.

19. Private email from Dr. Muldoon.

20. On this topic see, for example, R. S. Sugirtharajah, ed., *The Postcolonial Bible: The Bible and Postcolonialism* (Sheffield, England: Sheffield Academic Press, 1998); idem, *Decolonizing Biblical Texts: A View from the Margins* (Maryknoll, N.Y.: Orbis Books, 2000).

3. What Has Happened to the Study of the New Testament in the Last Forty Years?

Raymond F. Collins

The forty years that we celebrate, the forty years that have elapsed since the foundation of the graduate theology and pastoral ministry program at St. Michael's, have been four decades without precedent in the history of New Testament scholarship.

I. THE CONTEXT

The context in which this progress has been made is in many respects more important than the story of the advance itself. Notwithstanding the birth and growth of computer-assisted research, the study of the New Testament is essentially the work of humans. From humans come our knowledge of the New Testament; they are the source of our understanding.

A. From this perspective the Second Vatican Council (1962–65) marks a milestone in the history of New Testament scholarship. *Dei verbum* was one of only two dogmatic constitutions coming from the council. This document, with its encouragement for Catholic biblical scholars (par. 23) and its endorsement of form (par. 12) and redaction (par. 19) criticism marked a coming of age for Catholic biblical scholars. An early sign of this coming to maturity was the publication of *The Jerome Biblical Commentary*[1] under the leadership of Raymond E. Brown, Joseph A. Fitzmyer, and Roland Murphy. The appointment of Brown and Fitzmyer, as well as of Jerome Quinn to the Pontifical Biblical Commission[2] was a sign that Rome also recognized the coming of age of Catholic biblical scholarship in the United States.[3]

Almost as important for New Testament scholarship, not only for Roman Catholic scholars but also for scholars of other confessional persuasions, has been the ecumenical spirit fostered by the council. Its *Decree on Ecumenism* (*Unitatis Redintegratio*) recognized that "the written word of God" was the patrimony of all Christians (par. 3). In this spirit began the full partnership of Roman Catholic scholars in the study of the New Testament. The participation of Roman Catholics in the Society for New Testament Studies and the Society for Biblical Literature and the participation of scholars of other confessions in the Catholic Biblical Association bear ample witness to the new context in which the study of the New Testament is being conducted.

Striking proof of this new context is provided by the annual gatherings of the Society for New Testament Studies. Forty years ago it was a gentlemen's club of British Anglicans and German Lutherans. Now gatherings of the "club" have been turned into a virtual convention in which men and women, Africans and Japanese, French speakers and Dutch speakers, Catholics and Baptists all participate. The increased and more diversified pool that has resulted from this kind of interaction could only mean and did mean that the study of the New Testament was to make rapid strides as it breached the frontiers that were still so firmly established just forty years ago. The pool of New Testament scholars is interconfessional and intercontinental, male and female. To paraphrase the Pauline baptismal formula, "there is no longer Jew or Greek, there is no longer slave or free, there is no longer male and female" (Gal 3:28) in the study of the New Testament. Ethnic, class, and gender boundaries have been transcended in our common pursuit to understand more fully the New Testament.

B. The results of this broadening of interaction among scholars are evident. Allow me to cite as important witnesses to the effects of the new context two important publications. One is the *Greek New Testament*[4] under the auspices of the United Bible Societies. Its first edition (1966) was edited by Kurt Aland, Matthew Black, Bruce Metzger, and Allen Wikgren.[5] These scholars were preeminent in the study of various aspects of New Testament textual criticism, but the group did not include a single Roman Catholic. The second edition, published in 1968, listed the name of Carlo Martini, then of the Pontifical Biblical Institute in Rome and now cardinal-archbishop of Milan, as a member of the editorial board. The text of the third edition, published in 1975, was incorporated into the twenty-sixth edition of Nestle-Aland's *Novum Testamentum Graece*, published in 1979.[6] As of that date there exists a common edition of the New Testament text that is used throughout the world. It is the work of a group of scholars of several different confessional persuasions, speaking three different maternal tongues, living on two continents, but united in one edition of the New Testament of use to everyone.

The Jerome Biblical Commentary may be cited as a second example. Contributors to the first edition in 1968 were almost entirely American Roman Catholic clergy. Among the contributors to *The New Jerome Biblical Commentary*[7] published some twenty years later are both clergy and laypersons, including eight women. Three authors hail from Australia, two from Ireland, and one from Belgium. Let me note in passing that it was the rapid advances made in biblical studies during the twenty years in the center of our forty-year period that warranted the publication of the new edition. The original project, coming from the mideighties, was for a revision of the text. When it appeared, it was for the most part, almost two-thirds, an entirely new work.

The new context in which New Testament scholarship is taking place is reflected in the composition of the editorial board that has published the *New Revised Standard Version* of the Bible under the aegis of the National Council of Churches. It included Catholics and a Jew along with scholars belonging to the churches of the National Council. Editions of the NRSV now commonly include "the Apocrypha." Catholic editions of the NRSV follow the Roman tradition in the published sequence of the "Old Testament" books. The result is that the NRSV is the most commonly used English language text of the New Testament throughout the scholarly world.

Beyond texts and versions we can see the impact of this more comprehensive approach to the study of the New Testament in the publication of such tools of the trade as *The Anchor Bible Dictionary*[8] and *The Exegetical Dictionary of the New Testament (EDNT).*[9] Among the contributors to the first of the three volumes of the *EDNT* (1978) was just one woman (Luise Schottroff) and four non-continentals, two of whom were German expatriates. The second and third volumes would manifest a change of ratio. The hundreds—almost a full thousand—of contributors represent the full spectrum of contemporary biblical scholarship.

The cooperation of male and female scholars from different continents and with different confessional affiliations is reflected in the publication of the five major series of English-language commentaries on the Bible (or New Testament), as well as in the projected series of commentaries in the New Testament Library whose first volumes are already under way.[10] Those already published, but not yet completed, are The Anchor Bible, the Hermeneia series, the New International Greek Testament Commentaries, Sacra Pagina, and Word Biblical Commentaries.

It is otiose to cite one or another individual commentary as being a singularly important contribution to the advance of New Testament studies in the past four decades. Nonetheless, the commentaries by Brown on the Fourth Gospel and the Johannine Epistles and by Fitzmyer on Luke, Acts, and Romans in the Anchor Bible series have given a clear signal to the rest of the world of the coming of age of Roman Catholic biblical scholarship in the United States. It goes without saying that the name of Raymond Brown cannot be mentioned without some reference to *The Birth of the Messiah*[11] and *The Death of the Messiah*[12] that have appeared in the Anchor Bible Reference Library.

C. To mention the name of Joseph Fitzmyer without mentioning his study of the Dead Sea Scrolls would be to overlook an important, perhaps the most important, of his many contributions to New Testament scholarship. His participation in the publication of the monumental series known as Discoveries in the Judean Desert is just one example of how the discovery, publication, and cataloging of ancient manuscripts has changed the landscape of New Testament interpretation. Scholars presently have available for their use not only an increased number of manuscripts from Qumran but also manuscripts from an additional twelve sites in the Judean desert.[13]

No longer is the witness born by manuscripts such as the Dead Sea Scrolls considered as providing information about the "background" of the New Testament, the backdrop, as it were. Rather, these manuscripts, along with some limited archeological data, are to be seen as components of the environment or context to which the New Testament belongs. Some of these manuscripts provide linguistic keys that enable us to understand some elements of New Testament phraseology and a new angle of vision on the various religio-philosophical currents in New Testament times, including the mysterious world of Jewish apocalypticism.

As our focus moves from East to West, we must consider the discovery and publication of the Nag Hammadi codices. These have provided a new vista on the amorphous phenomenon known as Gnosticism so prevalent throughout the Eastern Mediterranean basin and its adjacent areas during the time in which the various books of the New Testament were written.

As a footnote to this observation, I should add that New Testament scholars not versed in Coptic now have some of the most important of the Nag Hammadi manuscripts available to them in James Robinson's *The Nag Hammadi Library*.[14] Along with the assistance provided by this popular edition of those ancient Gnostic manuscripts there should be noted two other valuable publications that have made the religious world of the New Testament more accessible to contemporary scholars: James Charlesworth's *Old Testament Pseudepigrapha*[15] and Hennecke-Schneemelcher's *New Testament Apocrypha*,[16] both collaborative efforts in two volumes.

D. Not to be overlooked in this rapid glance at discoveries and publications must certainly be the discovery and cataloging of texts of the New Testament. Without even mentioning ancient versions of the New Testament text, we must be aware of the increase in the number of papyri, majuscules, minuscules, and lectionary texts of the New Testament that have become available in the past forty years. Forty years ago Erwin Nestle had available for use in his preparation of the twenty-fifth edition of the *Novum Testamentum Graece* some 54 papyri, 206 majuscules, and 1074 minuscules.[17] Forty years later the editors of the fourth revised edition of *The Greek New Testament* (1993) were able to make use of 97 papyri, 300 majuscules, and 2464 minuscules. At the turn of the millennium available manuscripts of the Greek text included 115 papyri, 309 majuscules, 2862 minuscules, and 2412 lectionary texts.[18]

E. Mention of the manuscript materials presently available to scholars who are interested in the textual history of the New Testament brings us to a fifth element of the context within which New Testament study is presently conducted, so different from that of forty years ago. This is the technological age whose impact on the study of the New Testament can hardly be measured. Rather than attempt a complete survey of the new developments made possible by the technological revolution of the past few years, I would like simply to cite four specific contributions of technology to the study of the New Testament. The first is the use of photography in its increasingly sophisticated forms, which has allowed copies of manuscripts located in various libraries and museums throughout the world to be brought together in one place. A 1998 report on advances in New Testament textual research notes that photographic copies of papyri 100–115, majuscules 0307–0309, minuscule 1836, and lectionaries 2404, 2407–1410[19] were added to the collection in the Münster institute between 1995 and 1998. The institute now has available copies of more than six thousand New Testament manuscripts. What a far cry from the six manuscripts available to Erasmus when he prepared the *Textus Receptus*, the revered "Received Text"!

Second, computers are used today by virtually all New Testament scholars. To be sure, computer availability facilitates scholarly publication in various ways, including library research, but it also makes it possible for scholars to employ software that considerably improves research possibilities. To illustrate, one need only mention the availability of electronic copies of texts, versions, the *Komputerkonkordanz*, and of such reference works as *The Anchor Bible Dictionary* and the *Thesaurus Linguae Graece*.

Third, I must cite the contributions to New Testament scholarship of various electronic means of communication. As I prepared my commentary on 1 Corinthians,[20] I was grateful for the possibilities available to me to ask colleagues in Europe, Asia, Africa, and Australia for specific information, information that was generally made available to me within twenty-four hours of my initial query. On a broader scale, access to the Web has provided scholars with reviews of published literature, possibilities for discussion of certain issues,[21] and access to library catalogues.

In brief, the advent of this millennium, with its wider and ever more diversified pool of scholars; the discovery, cataloging, and publication of newly discovered manuscripts; and the ever expanding range of possibilities afforded by technological advances has created a context for New Testament study that is ever so different from the context in which I did my own doctoral research a short forty years ago.

II. METHODOLOGY

A. Forty years ago serious academic study of the New Testament was dominated by the use of the historical-critical method. Textual criticism had been on the scene for centuries. Form criticism had been developed by Schmidt, Dibelius, and Bultmann in the aftermath of the First World War. While the Second World War was still raging, the method of form criticism was endorsed by Pius XII for use by Roman Catholic scholars.[22] The aftermath of that war was such that it was not until the fifties that the methodology was used more universally and with increased enthusiasm and nuance in Roman Catholic circles.

At that very moment developments in the historical critical methodology were already on the horizon. In 1954 Willi Marxsen presented his doctoral thesis, later published in English with the title *Mark the Evangelist: Studies on the Redaction History of the Gospel*,[23] at the University of Kiel. In that same year a professor at the University of Zurich, Hans Conzelmann, published *The Theology of Saint Luke*,[24] the English title of a work whose German original was *Die Mitte der Zeit* (the center of time). These path-finding works rehabilitated Mark and Luke as authors and theologians in their own right. Mark and Luke could no longer be considered as mere compilers of earlier traditions. The "geography" and "history" of their respective "gospels" were not what they had seemed to be. Geography and history were used, even created by the evangelists, to present a theological vision of the ministry of Jesus of Nazareth.

The synoptic trilogy was completed in 1960 when Günther Bornkamm published some of his own work, along with the doctoral research of two of his students, Gerhard Barth and Heinz Joachim Held, as *Tradition and Interpretation in Matthew*.[25] As of that time it has been clear that the Matthean gospel is as much the story of a church as it is the story of Jesus. During the next forty years it would become increasingly clear that the Matthean church was a Jewish community trying to make its own way in a Jewish world that had collapsed in the wake of the destruction of Jerusalem.

During the years that followed the publication of the Marxsen-Conzelmann-Bornkamm trilogy the method was refined, both as redaction criticism and as emendation criticism, so that ever new insights, both historical and theological, were able to be gleaned from the gospel stories about Jesus.

B. In Pauline studies a consensus emerged shortly before the beginning of the 1990s that considered six of the Pauline epistles—Ephesians, Colossians, 2 Thessalonians, 1–2 Timothy, and Titus—as unauthentic. That left the remaining seven letters to be grouped together and studied under the rubric of the "undisputed Pauline letters." Throughout the last forty years these seven letters were increasingly viewed through a historical prism with the result that Paul can no longer be considered as a theologian with a ready-made corpus of doctrines. He must be seen as a theologian who was doing theology *currente calamo.*

From the standpoint of methodology, Pauline studies have been considerably enriched by the development of epistolary criticism. Three names come immediately to the fore as having made singular contributions to this development. The first is Heikki Koskenniemi, whose 1956 study on the ideas and phraseology of Hellenistic letters[26] came to the ken of other than Scandinavian scholars in the ensuing decades. His work on the triple function of a letter as mediating the presence of the writer, evoking the relationship among the parties, and conveying a specific message has proved to be of singular importance in the analysis of Paul's correspondence. A second name is that of Abraham Malherbe, whose work on the Pseudo-Demetrius and the Pseudo-Libanius[27] has enabled New Testament scholars to study Paul's letters in the light of Hellenistic epistolary categories. Finally, one must mention the work of James White, whose publication of Hellenistic papyri letters[28] moved the turn-of-the century efforts of Adolf Deissman to a phase where copies of Hellenistic letters were made available to Pauline scholars, who profited from a comparison between the work of Paul and that of other Hellenistic letter writers.

These pioneering efforts have enabled scholars to appreciate more fully Paul's letters as the occasional correspondence that they really were. In addition to standard considerations of epistolary form—the Hellenistic letter is a distinct literary form!—there are epistolary cliches and epistolary conventions to be observed in the way that Paul wrote to the churches in Thessalonica and Corinth. There is, moreover, a whole range of considerations appropriately grouped together under the rubric of epistolary hermeneutics that are truly significant for the interpretation of Paul's writings when they are considered as real letters.

Epistolary considerations are also significant for the understanding of the post-Pauline letters, both those written in Paul's name and those attributed to other authors. Specifically, one can note the importance of epistolary considerations in imparting additional nuance to the various issues surrounding the deutero-Paulines.

C. The fact that the art of letter writing was something that was taught and learned in the rhetorical schools draws attention to the importance of rhetorical criticism as a means of better understanding Paul's letters. Once again three names come immediately to the fore as pioneers in the use of this methodology in Pauline studies: George Kennedy, a classicist; Wilhelm Wuellner; and Margaret M. Mitchell. Kennedy's principal contribution was to urge New Testament scholars to identify the rhetorical genre of the text to be interpreted. Wuellner added additional nuance to the question of rhetorical genre. He used as a point of departure the New Testament texts rather than the ancient categories.

Weaknesses in some attempts to use rhetorical criticism in New Testament study have included an all too mechanical application of the ancient categories to New Testament literature. Some of these attempts seem almost to presume that Paul, as a student in class, had a handbook of forensic rhetoric at his side as he wrote his letters. In fact, the classic categories have something of the character of a static abstraction. In real life the use of categories is much more supple. So it is with Paul's letters.

Margaret Mitchell's major contribution to the use of rhetorical criticism came in the form of her doctoral thesis on 1 Corinthians, *Paul and the Rhetoric of Reconciliation*,[29] in which she determined that 1 Corinthians 1:10 was the major thesis (the *prothesis*) of the entire letter. Such highlighting of Paul's plea for unity and of his use of more than one classic rhetorical trope in the development of his argument has enabled recent scholars to look at this letter in a new light, with much greater clarity than had previously been possible.

To be sure, ancient rhetoric, and perhaps even more important the so-called new rhetoric, have proved useful for the analysis of New Testament literature other than the epistles of Paul. In my opinion, however, what rhetorical criticism has contributed to the understanding of New Testament letters far surpasses the contribution that it has made to gospel criticism, in the narrow sense of the study of the four canonical gospels.[30]

D. The advances in Pauline studies made possible by the use of rhetorical criticism are paralleled by the contributions made by narrative criticism to the understanding of the New Testament's short stories that have Jesus as their subject. As with the application of rhetorical criticism to the New Testament's epistolary literature, it is useful to distinguish between the somewhat static and abstract contributions of the structuralists with their Proppian analysis of the "deep structure" of a narrative and the more supple contributions made by North American narratologists.

The latter, among whom the name of Jack Dean Kingsbury comes readily to mind, have advanced the understanding of the gospels with their considerations of plot, scene, characterization, and narrative time—to mention but a few of the foci to which a narrative study of the gospel texts draws particular attention. One can think of the work of Beverly Roberts Gaventa and Pheme Perkins, whose respective works on Mary and Simon Peter have highlighted the characterization of each of these figures by those New Testament authors who wrote about them in their stories about Jesus.[31]

Reflecting on the importance of narrative criticism one should also include as a corollary or perhaps under the rubric of meta-narrativity reader response criticism and the use of such categories as implied author, implied reader, and so forth. Many have profited from the use of this kind of analysis in understanding how the New Testament narratives convey their meaning. Since the narratives have been passed down to us in the form of text, I would be remiss were I not to mention Ricoeur's seminal work on textuality as having made its own significant contribution to New Testament study.

E. In the past four decades a plethora of methodologies have been developed or tentatively advanced as being useful for a fuller understanding of the New Testament. The good exegete, unlike the good writer of a doctoral dissertation, is one who employs all these various methodologies in a creative tension so as allow the text to yield its full measure of intelligibility.[32] I prefer not to gainsay the value of any of these methodologies, but I must add that some methods are ultimately more useful than others.

In addition to the four methodologies that have already been highlighted I feel obliged to signal out an additional two methods that have generated a great deal of press, much criticism, and not a few best sellers in recent years. Each of these methods is not so much a method of study as it is a way of approaching the New Testament text. Thus, we can speak of a social or sociological reading and of a feminist reading of the New Testament texts. The mere mention of each of these kinds of readings surely elicits a full range and full measure of audience response criticism, but these readings must not be overlooked if we are to appreciate the advances made in New Testament study during the past forty years.

The rubric of the social/sociological reading of the New Testament embraces a wide variety of endeavors. Three types of approach deserve particular mention. The first consists of the attention that has been paid to the social location of the communities for which the various New Testament texts have been written. Among those who have used this approach, albeit in different fashion, are John Elliott, who studied 1 Peter as addressed to a community in physical exile, and Gerd Theissen, who has considered the church at Corinth as a community torn by divisions between the rich and the poor, the haves and the have-nots.[33]

The second approach is one that focuses on vocabulary that has a social connotation. To illustrate, I draw attention to the importance of the household and the use of kinship language in the writings of the New Testament. When I was a young student, exegesis paid virtually no attention to the fact that early Christian communities gathered in households, necessarily limited in size and governed by the social conventions of the times. To cite but one more example—and many could be cited—one must look at the institution of slavery and how it has influenced the New Testament texts. Spanning these two examples is certainly the use of the *Haustafeln,* the household codes of the New Testament. The household code is a literary form, but it was virtually overlooked in early twentieth-century form criticism. It is, however, an extremely important literary form in a social/sociological reading of some of the New Testament texts.[34]

A third approach considers Jesus in the guise of a wandering cynic and the locus of the development of the Jesus movement in Mediterranean peasant society. The many works, sometimes repetitive, of John Dominic Crossan are certainly the most widely known illustrations of this approach to New Testament study, but professional students of the New Testament are well aware that Crossan's works are but an extreme example of a broader approach.

F. If I have left the feminist reading of the New Testament until last it is not because it is of least importance; it is rather because a feminist reading of the scriptures touches the roots of some aspects of narrative criticism and of the social/sociological reading of the text. I readily grant that a feminist reading of the New Testament is a byproduct of the feminist movement in society at large. It is, nonetheless, a legitimate and valuable method of reading the text. As a method, it has close links, often overlooked, with other methods of New Testament study.

As was the case with the social/sociological reading of the text, a feminist reading of the New Testament embraces a wide variety of approaches. Some years ago Mary Ann Tolbert published an article in *Semeia* that distinguished among three types of feminist reading.[35] I would call these three a prophetic reading, an intense reading, and a deconstructionist reading of the text. The first looks at various passages within the New Testament that are critical of society as it is. The second looks at and explores passages that speak of women and women's concerns but that have been overlooked by a hitherto male-dominated scholarly guild. Dare I say that Elisabeth Schüssler Fiorenza's *In Memory of Her*[36] provided the manifesto for this type of approach? Finally there is a third type of feminist of the text that calls for a radical revision of early Christianity in the light of its patriarchal structures. I fear that it is this latter type of approach that provoked the caveat attached to the discussion of the feminist reading in the Pontifical Biblical Commission's *The Interpretation of the Bible in the Church*.[37] Notwithstanding the document's extreme caution, a feminist reading of the New Testament allows us to appreciate the Magdalene and Phoebe, respectively so important for the ministry of Jesus and of Paul, in a way that we could not have understood these evangelists some forty years ago.

III. CONCLUSIONS

As I draw near to my conclusion I must express my gratitude to the organizers of the anniversary symposium. Their project of a forty-year survey was less ambitious than the various centenary projects undertaken by the editors of *Time* a year ago. For that I am so thankful.

In my rapid survey of the past forty years of New Testament study I have attempted to get to the heart of the matter in examining the study of the New Testament by examining the changing context and the development of new methodologies in the past four decades. Much more can be said about recent New Testament scholarship, but I would like to conclude my overview of the past forty years by highlighting four areas in which significant advance has taken place as a result of the new context, the development of new methodologies, and the refinement of older methodologies.

A. A first would be the third quest for the historical Jesus. At the beginning of our four-decade period the so-called second quest for the historical Jesus was beginning to make its mark on the scene of New Testament scholarship. The past decade has seen tremendous strides in our efforts to understand the life and ministry of Jesus of Nazareth, the historical figure of two millennia past. These various efforts can be considered together under the rubric of the third quest for the historical Jesus, the Jesus of history. John Meier's series on Jesus, titled *A Marginal Jew,* can be considered as a highlight of this new quest.[38]

B. A second area to be mentioned is the movement that has taken place in the study of the synoptic problem. For all practical purposes the so-called modified-two-source theory must now be considered as virtually axiomatic in synoptic studies. Given the priority of Mark, Matthew and Luke can be considered as new revised editions of the Markan story. Synoptic criticism has matured to the point at which it is now possible to consider Matthew and Luke as truly creative works by gifted authors who used their individual literary talents and developed their own agendas. From this perspective one must highlight the fact that Matthew's gospel is a Jewish story, written for a group of (Christian) Jews among those other Jews who were trying to define themselves in relationship to Scripture and to one another after the destruction of Jerusalem. From a similar perspective, Luke's gospel is to be seen as part one of a Hellenistic historical narrative in two parts.

C. While the matter of the sources of the Fourth Gospel continues to be of interest to many scholars, the real strides in Johannine studies seem to revolve around the community of the Beloved Disciple. J. Louis Martyn and Raymond Brown led the way to this community.[39] Others continue to follow. We cannot, however, speak of the Fourth Gospel without recognizing that a perennial question has been the identity of the (human) authority on which it is based, that of the Beloved Disciple himself (herself?). In the quest for the Beloved Disciple, James Charlesworth's monumental *The Beloved Disciple* is the newest guide.[40]

D. The coming of a new millennium at the conclusion of four decades of New Testament scholarship raised much apocalyptic speculation. Can one conclude a survey of New Testament scholarship without noting Käsemann's interest in Paul's apocalypticism? And the publications of Jewish apocalyptic writings that have marked the past forty years? I think not. So allow me to conclude my survey by expressing the hope that as we move into this new millennium we might be better able to appreciate the enigma that is the Book of Revelation.

NOTES

1. Raymond E. Brown, Joseph A. Fitzmyer, and Roland Murphy, eds., *The Jerome Biblical Commentary* (Englewood Cliffs, N.J.: Prentice-Hall, 1968).

2. In a survey of this sort I can but note the significance of two publications of the Pontifical Biblical Commission, namely, *The Instruction on the Historical Truth of the Gospels* (1964) and *The Interpretation of the Bible in the Church* (1993).

3. Given the audience for which this essay is intended, the examples cited will be skewed in favor of the American and Roman Catholics with whom the audience is presumed to be familiar.

4. Kurt Aland et al., *The Greek New Testament* (New York: American Bible Society; London: British and Foreign Bible Society, 1966).

5. Arthur Voobus also participated in the early phases of the committee's work.

6. Kurt Aland et al., eds., *Novum Testamentum Graece*, 26th ed (Stuttgart: Deutsche Bibelstiftung, 1979).

7. Raymond E. Brown, Joseph A. Fitzmyer, and Roland E. Murphy, eds., *The New Jerome Biblical Commentary* (Englewood Cliffs, N.J.: Prentice-Hall, 1990).

8. David Noel Freedman, editor-in-chief, *The Anchor Bible Dictionary,* 6 vols. (New York: Doubleday, 1992).

9. Horst Balz and Gerhard Schneider, *Exegetical Dictionary of the New Testament,* 3 vols. (Grand Rapids, Mich.: Eerdmans, 1990–93).

10. The first volumes appeared in the fall of 2001.

11. Raymond E. Brown, *The Birth of the Messiah: A Commentary on the Infancy Narratives in Matthew and Luke* (New York: Doubleday, 1993). An updated edition in 1993 was included in the ABRL series.

12. Raymond E. Brown, *The Death of the Messiah: From Gethsemane to the Grave: A Commentary on the Passion Narrativies in the Four Gospels,* 2 vols. (New York: Doubleday, 1994).

13. See the list in Patrick H. Alexander et al., eds., *The SBL Handbook of Style: For Ancient Near Eastern Biblical, and Early Christian Studies* (Peabody, Mass.: Hendrickson, 1999), 177. This handbook is a valuable tool and itself a witness to the increasingly cooperative nature of New Testament studies.

14. James Robinson, *The Nag Hammadi Library in English* (Leiden: E. J. Brill, 1977).

15. James Charlesworth, *Old Testament Pseudepigrapha,* 2 vols. (Garden City, N.Y.: Doubleday, 1983, 1985).

16. Wilhelm Schneemelcher, *New Testament Apocrypha,* 2 vols. (Philadelphia: Westminister, 1963–66). These two volumes were originally published in German in 1959 and 1964.

17. These figures are collated from the 1954 printing of the *Novum Testamentum Graece,* which I used at the time of my doctoral studies.

18. Cf. *Bericht der Hermann Kunst-Stiftung zur Forderung der neutestamentlichen Textforschung fur die Jahre 1995 bis 1998* (Munster: Regenensberg Munster, 1998), 14–18.

19. *Bericht der Textforschung fur die Jahre 1995 bis 1998,* 18.

20. Raymond F. Collins, *First Corinthians* (Collegeville, Minn.: Liturgical Press, 1999).

21. For example, the Johannine Discussion Group.

22. See the encyclical letter *Divino afflante Spiritu,* 30 September 1943.

23. Willi Marxsen, *Mark the Evangelist: Studies on the Redaction History of the Gospel* (Nashville, Tenn.: Abingdon Press, 1969).

24. Hans Conzelmann, *The Theology of Saint Luke* (New York: Harper, 1961).

25. Günther Bornkamm, Gerhard Barth, and Heinz Joachim Held, *Tradition and Interpretation in Matthew* (Philadelphia: Westminister, 1963).

26. Heikki Koskenniemi, *Studien zur Idee und Phraseologie des griechischen Briefes bis 400 n. Chr.* (Helsinki: 1956).

27. Abraham Malherbe, *Ancient Epistolary Theorists,* Sources for Biblical Studies 19 (Atlanta: The Scholars Press, 1988).

28. James White, *Light from Ancient Letters,* Foundations and Facets (Philadelphia: Fortress Press, 1986).

29. Margaret Mitchell, *Paul and the Rhetoric of Reconciliation: An Exegetical Investigation of the Language and Composition of 1 Corinthians* (Tübingen: Mohr, 1991).

30. I have argued that the letters of Paul must be considered as "the gospel according to Paul" (see *Preaching of the Epistles* [New York: Paulist Press, 1996]).

31. Beverly Roberts Gaventa, *Mary: Glimpses of the Mother of Jesus* (Columbia, S.C.: University of South Carolina Press, 1995); Pheme Perkins, *Peter: Apostle for the Whole Church* (Columbia, S.C.: University of South Carolina Press, 1994).

32. In fact, the various methodologies used in the study of the New Testament are not always radically distinct from one another. While acknowledging that the use of form criticism was first applied to the Synoptic Gospels, one can certainly argue that epistolary criticism is merely another name for the form criticism of the letters.

33. John H. Elliot, *A Home for the Homeless: A Social-scientific Criticism of 1 Peter, Its Situation and Strategy* (Minneapolis, Minn.: Fortress Press, 1990); Gerd Theissn, *The Social Setting of Pauline Christianity: Essays on Corinth* (Philadelphia: Fortress Press, 1982).

34. One should not overlook the importance of a social/sociological reading of the New Testament for understanding New Testament ecclesiology.

35. Mary Ann Tolbert, "Defining the Problem: The Bible and Feminist Hermeneutics," *Semeia* 28 (1983), 113–26.

36. Elisabeth Schüssler Fiorenza, *In Memory of Her: A Feminist Theological Reconstruction of Christian Origins* (New York: Crossroad, 1983).

37. The English translation was published on 6 January 1994 in *Origins* 23/29. The document had officially been published a few months earlier.

38. John Meier, *A Marginal Jew: Rethinking the Historical Jesus*, 3 vols. (New York: Doubleday, 1991, 1994). Volume 4 is expected to be published at a later date.

39. See J. Louis Martyn, *History and Theology in the Fourth Gospel* (New York: Harper & Row, 1968); Raymond Brown, *The Community of the Beloved Disciple* (New York: Paulist Press, 1979).

40. James Charlesworth, *The Beloved Disciple: Whose Witness Validates the Gospel of John* (Valley Forge, Pa.: Trinity Press International, 1995).

4. Some Trends in American Catholic Systematic Theology Since 1965

Michael A. Fahey

It is a pleasure to participate in this Reunion 2000 anniversary celebration for the graduate theology and pastoral ministry program. From 1978 through 1986 I spent busy summers here as a professor. St. Michael's hospitality was often channelled through the Edmundites and specifically through Father Paul Couture. The graduate theology faculty always felt at home here. We shared in the liturgical, cultural, and community life of St. Michael's. Over the years I have borrowed many of St. Michael's ideas about creating a summer community of learning and faith. I certainly learned more here than I ever taught. The program remains for me an ongoing source of inspiration and hope even in times when I feel disappointed at the pace of reform in our church.

My chapter is dedicated to the late Betty Rafoul. During the summers I taught here (when for many of us courses were taught for six weeks) Betty was the heart of the program. She inspired us with her thoughtfulness and efficiency; Betty and her husband Gerry annually invited the graduate faculty to their home for a gourmet dinner. It is hard to imagine the stunning successes of this program in those years and later without her presence. I am sure she is smiling down at us right now, and wishing that we would skip all the fuss being made about her.

The American Academy of Religion and the Society of Biblical Literature several years ago initiated a popular feature for conventions at which senior members are asked to speak about how their mind has changed in the last twenty years. My presentation follows something of that literary genre. But I am speaking about how my church has evolved since 1965, especially in its dealings with theologians, and second, how Catholic theology has shifted in the United States during the last thirty-five years. I choose as my terminus a quo 1965, the year of the closing of

Vatican II. My task is a tall order indeed, one that can be treated only in broad strokes. I share with you how I see the overall picture, one that has not always been rosy. But I speak out of a love for the church that has been my hearth and home all my life. Much of what I touch upon obviously needs fuller nuancing, but this is not the place for a book-length presentation.

To give some order to my remarks I distinguish between two issues:

A. *How have elements in the Roman Catholic Church changed since 1965—especially the leadership structures relating to the theological community, realities that invite praise or concern?*

B. *What are the ongoing accomplishments within American Catholic systematic theology since 1965?*

While the issues are interrelated, they are not identical. Listening to several presentations at the June 2000 annual meeting of the Catholic Theological Society of America in San Jose, I felt that some theologians were overlooking this distinction and acting as though critique of ecclesial structures were the principal (dare I say only) task of the theological enterprise.

A. SIX NOTABLE CHANGES IN ROMAN CATHOLIC CHURCH LIFE SINCE 1965

1. First of all, it is clear that internationally the papacy has never before possessed such a high profile or exercised such a centralist form of governance as it does now. This shift is somewhat ironic and unexpected since Vatican II was conceived by many as a council to enhance the role of bishops and to highlight the notion of collegiality. The present pontiff, John Paul II, has a distinguished record of thoughtful pronouncements that illustrate his role as a charismatic and prophetic teacher, especially in various areas of social concern. The increased focus on the papacy, enhanced notably by the pope's international trips, has highlighted the multicultural life of Catholicism. These papal trips, despite their enormous cost, in some instances (especially in

Canada) moved bishops' conferences during the preparatory stages to tap the ideas of the faithful, as bishops worked on drafts of speeches for the pope to deliver on the spot. But generally the papal visits, including those that featured encounters with Catholic youth, seem to have had only ephemeral impact on church life because of their baroque ambience.

Likewise, the increasingly close supervision and scrutiny by the pope, working through the Roman curial offices, in the selection of bishops have resulted in the appointment of bishops who are reluctant to take prophetic stances that could be interpreted as lack of loyalty to the Holy See. Never before in the history of the Catholic Church, not even under Pope Pius IX, has the papacy held such a controlling command over the church universal.

2. Closely connected with that phenomenon, in the last fifteen years or so there has been a diminishment in the teaching office of bishops, specifically through episcopal conferences. After a rush of creative initiatives and impressive publications by national conferences in the 1970s and 1980s, the 1990s saw a loss of courage and venturesomeness. The Holy See has asserted that documents of national episcopal conferences are not vehicles for the ordinary magisterium of the church. The NCCB/USCC, the Canadian Conference of Catholic Bishops, Conférence épiscopale de France, CELAM, the Bishops' Conference of England and Wales, to name only a few, after a spate of stunning documents (one thinks of the U.S. bishops' statements on morality in economic life or on peace, both of which were the products of meticulous listening and consultation) have become relatively silent. Hence, in areas where there is need for local guidance tailored to national needs, the collective voice of bishops has diminished. I mention only two examples of concern: the church's need for improved relations with women and appropriate pastoral care of lesbians and gays.

Another example of diminishment in the teaching office of the bishops is the International Synod of Bishops. These synods were initially designed after Vatican II by Pope Paul VI and leading council bishops to promote closer cooperation between the Petrine ministry and the ministry of bishops. By the 1980s the synods had become so closely orchestrated by centralized Roman control of their themes, prepared *lineamenta,* subsequent *instrumenta laboris,* and even final documents (formulated subsequently as post-synodal apostolic [papal] exhortations), that these synods lost much of their potential for sharing information, free discussion, and choosing pastoral options.

3. A third phenomenon, again closely related to the first two, has been a cooling relationship between the papal/episcopal leadership and many theologians, especially theologians attempting to assist the church to dialogue more effectively with the modern world and to come up with alternate ways of formulating the church's teachings. I am not referring here to the more dramatic "dressings down" and in a few cases removal of a teaching *mandatum* such as in the case of Hans Küng, Charles Curran, Leonardo Boff, Edward Schillebeeckx, Jacques Dupuis, and Anthony de Mello. I refer rather to a more generalized breakdown in dialogue between theologians and members of the hierarchy—bishops and pope. This cooling helps to explain the unease of the majority of American Catholic theologians to the specific rules for implementing *Ex corde ecclesiae* in the United States.

Let me give you what I consider to be a paradigm example of this shift. Recently, in preparing a paper on the role of Mary in God's design, I had occasion to reread chapter 8 of *Lumen gentium:* "The Role of the Blessed Virgin Mary, Mother of God, in the Mystery of Christ and the Church." You recall that there had been a push among some council fathers to have a separate and expansive constitution on Mary. Instead, it was decided to have the Marian teachings placed in a chapter of *Lumen gentium* on the church. In that chapter the bishops stated their decision to integrate Marian doctrine and piety into the role of the church, "without intending to put forward a complete doctrine of Mary or of settling questions which have not yet been brought fully to light through the work of theologians" (no. 54). In other words, the bishops explained that they were waiting for theologians to complete their research before they, the bishops, would feel authorized to make further statements on the prerogatives of Mary. It is difficult to imagine that sentence about collaboration being written today.

During the council, at afternoon and evening discussions, and on a variety of committees, theological *periti* (not all of the same leanings) worked closely with the bishops, helping them to understand the issues, and even drafting for the bishops various speeches and conciliar texts. Today, I regret to say, that level of cooperation with theologians is rare, except among a very narrow circle of chosen theologians or with the man called the pope's "personal theologian." Fortunately, there are a few exceptions.

In 1986 Karl Rahner described this estrangement between bishops and theologians in the German edition of *Faith in a Wintry Season*.[1] For Rahner, the Catholic Church was passing through a time of winter. In a similar vein, the late Richard McCormick wrote of a "chill factor" blowing through the Catholic Church.[2] A new phenomenon emerged, namely interpreting theologians' disagreement on non-defined doctrinal teachings as dissent and not legitimate prophetic invitation by theologians to official teachers to be more comprehensive in how they communicate "official" teachings. Especially in the 1980s the word *dissent* came to be demonized as an activity inimical to the church, a lack of *obsequium religiosum* toward authoritative statements emanating from papal or curial teachings. Pope John Paul II's motu proprio *Ad tuendam fidem* (dated 18 May 1998) on protecting the church from the errors of theologians, and several days later his document *Apostolos suos* on the "Theological and Juridical Nature of Episcopal Conferences" (dated 21 May 1998) gave canonical force to these attitudes of alienation vis-à-vis theologians.

Several years ago Yves Congar noted the shifting meaning associated with the term *magisterium*. He showed that in the church before the mid-nineteenth century the term meant "teachership" or "the activity of *magistri*—professors, bishops, various experts." Eventually the Latin term *magisterium* (which has neither a definite nor indefinite article, that is, does it mean *a* magisterium, or *the* magisterium?) took on the meaning of "that specific person or group of persons whose ministry in the church privileged them to teach authoritatively." The term became *magisterium authenticum*, and the Latin word *authenticum* is widely mistranslated into English as "authentic" when it actually means "authoritative."[3]

4. Another notable change since 1965 has been the shift in the profile of theologians. What occurred was a shift away from seminaries—where theology was studied by future priests—to university graduate programs in Catholic theology for a much wider constituency of theological students, at least half of whom are lay, sometimes more than half of whom are women. This created a Copernican shift in regard to who does theology and what ecclesial experiences enter the crucible of theology. This is seen most notably in moral theology, which is no

longer studied primarily by priests to assess the species and gravity of confessed sins but now has a far broader purpose. While some free-standing seminaries are still in operation, they are complemented by the divinity schools, sometimes in ecumenical consortia, and they are quite distinct from graduate programs in theology taught at universities. Marquette University was the first Catholic university in the United States to design a doctoral program in theology specifically for laypersons; a number of other Catholic universities in the United States followed suit.

The emergence of women Catholic theologians has occurred at a speed we have not yet fully appreciated. What would be the face of American Catholic theology today without the insights of Elisabeth Schüssler Fiorenza, Elizabeth Johnson, Mary Catherine Hilkert, Margaret Farley, Katarina Schuth, to name only a few? Walter Burghardt, my predecessor for many years as editor-in-chief of the journal *Theological Studies*, recently noted the shifts in the face of U.S. Catholic theology in his autobiography, *Long Have I Loved Thee: A Theologian Reflects on His Church*, by showing that, in its first decade of existence, authors publishing in *Theological Studies* were men, nearly all of whom were teaching in seminaries. Between 1940 and 1949, 144 articles published in *Theological Studies* came from seminary professors, only 41 from colleges; in the decade just completed, the 1990s, 44 articles came from seminaries or divinity schools, and 234 from colleges or universities. Since I took over as editor of *Theological Studies* in 1996, every issue has included at least one article by a woman theologian.

5. The most notable success story of the last thirty-five years has been, in my view, the involvement of Catholic theologians in the international and national bilateral ecumenical consultations among various churches in response to the mandate of Vatican II to promote the reunion of churches. These consultations, especially the Lutheran/Roman Catholic International, the Anglican/Roman Catholic International Commission, and nationally the U.S. Lutheran/Roman Catholic Dialogue, the Group of Les Dombes (Reformed/Catholics in French-speaking Europe), as well as the multiconfessional Faith and Order Commission of the World Council of Churches (in which Catholics serve as full, active members) have produced an impressive array of theological consensus statements that have contextualized longstanding griefs between churches and creatively expressed in new language the Christian tradition handed down to us from the apostles. These documents have set a

high standard for theological exchange and discourse. It is hard to imagine any course in sacramental theology not including a study of the Faith and Order's Lima document, *Baptism, Eucharist, Ministry*, or a course in ecclesiology that would not make use of the text of the *Groupe des Dombes* (for the conversion of the churches). These ecumenical consensus statements show how important it is for theologians and others to listen to one another, to accept criticism and puzzlement as helpful instruments, and to commit one's church to the discovery of new ways of responding to the signs of the times.

For theologians, however, one troubling feature regarding these ecumenical documents is that those in positions of authority in the Catholic Church almost never draw upon these texts in their own published statements. There is a notable reluctance on their part to "receive" these texts as faithful expressions of the tradition of the church. Nonetheless, the Pontifical Council for Promoting Christian Unity has the best track record of all the Roman curial offices in terms of openness and willingness to participate with other churches as equal partners.

6. Finally, there has been a decline in broader dissemination of Catholic culture since the 1960s, and certainly even more notably than since the 1940s. The reasons for this are not altogether clear. In part, I think, it is related to the decline in Catholic elementary and secondary school enrollments. Programs for religious education of post-confirmation Catholic youth also seem to be down. The appropriate stress on scripture-based homilies for the eucharistic liturgy has eliminated one opportunity for hearing teaching that used to occur (at least in some parishes) at Masses and paraliturgical devotions. Catholic bookstores are a rarity in most U.S. (and even German) cities. Fortunately, we have some Catholic book clubs, and web-based suppliers such as Amazon.com are available. But how many of our parishes provide enlightened pamphlets, booklets, newspapers, and books at the rear of the church? Here the British Catholic Church outshines us by leagues. Most U.S. diocesan newspapers seem more like house organs; the weakest ones are simply reports on the activities of the local ordinary and clergy appointments. Our theology graduates have not been hired by the staffs of newspapers (Catholic or secular); we do not support the shrinking number of publishers still struggling to make a living. Fortunately, we have, among others, Paulist Press, Liturgical Press, Orbis Books, Ignatius

Press, and now ecumenical publishers such as Fortress Press and Eerdmans. There remain some enlightened Catholic weeklies and monthlies, including the London *Tablet,* which has a notable North American circulation. There are also a few national Catholic newspapers, but they continue to be read only by those sympathetic to their editorial vision and priorities. They are not places where the polarized sectors of the American Catholic interact.

Compared to the pre–Vatican II days when I entered the Jesuit novitiate, there is a notable decline in the number of theological works translated from French and German. Perhaps one of the effects of inculturation is that readers are less interested in trends elsewhere. Latin American theology does appeal to some readership. Translators are hard to find, and they are notoriously underpaid for thankless work. Do our parishes support any reading and discussion clubs? Are there still parishes where there are biblical circles devoted to the study of a book of the Bible? Has the *Catechism of the Catholic Church* had any impact on restoring Catholic culture and promoting reading habits?

I do not see much trickle-down information or insights going from highly trained people to the ordinary parishioner. Often there is more involvement in social justice movements than in reading more academic issues. Our parishes do not promote in-depth lecture series, although "missions" are still offered in some parishes.

B. AMERICAN CATHOLIC SYSTEMATIC THEOLOGY: SOME TRENDS SINCE 1965

1. With the ever-increasing complexity of systematic theology and its demand for mastery of considerable historical and doctrinal detail, it is not surprising that a comprehensive dogmatic theology by one author seems to be fast becoming a thing of the past. Two of the most successful overviews of systematics in recent time have been collaborative works: *Systematic Theology: Roman Catholic Perspectives* and *Initiation à la pratique de la théologie.*[4] Neither could have been written by one person. Earlier attempts at a complete systematic theology by one person, such as Juan-Luis Segundo, Wolfhart Pannenberg, or Michael Schmaus, pale by comparison. None of the recently deceased

giants of Catholic systematic theology attempted a comprehensive systematic organon on their own: Bernard Lonergan (d. 1984), Karl Rahner (d. 1984), Hans Urs von Balthasar (d. 1988), Yves Congar (d. 1995), or Richard McCormick (d. 2000).

At the comprehensive level, among the most helpful works in U.S. Catholic theology in the past two decades have been the collaborative theological dictionaries such as *The New Dictionary of Theology*, *The New Dictionary of Sacramental Worship*, *The New Dictionary of Catholic Spirituality*, and the *HarperCollins Encyclopedia of Catholicism*.[5] Thus, the fruit of the last thirty-five years has not been all-inclusive systematic treatises by one person but rather individual monographs relating to a very specific subdiscipline.

In the interest of brevity, I restrict my overview to some important developments in systematic theology in three main areas: ecclesiology, Christology/Trinity, and Eucharist. I point only to monographs, even though I fully recognize that journal articles often anticipate by ten years or so research that is gestating. Finally, I touch briefly on a few areas of theology that show particular promise of rapid expansion in the near future.

1. Ecclesiology. The twentieth century, especially its last one-third, was the century of ecclesiology. Among Catholics and other Christians in dialogue with Catholics there was a flowering of this subdiscipline. Thanks to the impact of redaction-criticism of the gospels, there ensued a multiplicity of studies showing ecclesial diversities within the New Testament communities themselves. Here I think of the pioneering work of Raymond Brown: *The Community of the Beloved Disciple* (1979); *The Churches the Apostles Left Behind* (1984); and, with John P. Meier, *Antioch and Rome* (1983). I think also of Wayne A. Meeks, whose *The First Urban Christians* (1983) achieved a comparable synthesis of the Pauline material. Interest in the sociocultural life of the early Christian communities became the topic of numerous studies, preeminently by Gerd Theissen. These books showed the subtle interplay between the worldwide (universal) church and the local churches of the Mediterranean world. These works fleshed out what Vatican II had asserted about the universal church being truly present (*vere adest*) in the local churches.

The work of Avery Dulles, especially in the 1970s and 1980s, set a high standard of excellence. Few books in ecclesiology have had more impact than *Models of the Church* (1974, revised in 1987). This was followed by a host of other ecclesiological studies, among which one should mention *A Church to Believe In* (1982), and *The Catholicity of the Church* (1985).

Renewed interest in the "local" churches gradually shifted, partly at the request of the Vatican, to adapt that terminology to a consideration of "particular" churches. The classic treatment of particular churches in their interaction with the church universal is the magisterial study by Jean-Marie Tillard, O.P., titled *Église d'Églises: L'ecclésiologie de communion* (1987).[6] Tillard drew in part upon a significant corpus of material on *koinonia* developed in various ecumenical settings such as the bilateral conversations and projects of the World Council of Churches.

Liberation theology, especially its stress on inculturation and conscientization, also affected ecclesiology. The influence of individuals such as Paulo Freire was evident even in CELAM's Medellín conference of 1968, which marked a high point of creative interaction between liberation theology and ecclesiology. A further contribution emerged through the Ecumenical Association of Third World Theologians (EAT-WOT), all of whose works were quickly published in English by Orbis Books.

Expanding on insights raised by Cardinal Suenens and others at Vatican II regarding charisms in the church, theological studies on the charisms of ministries, both ordained and lay, emerged in ecclesiological works. A straight line of influence can be traced from ecumenical documents such as the Lima document and the ARCIC final report on ministry. Numerous works on the Petrine ministry, or papal office, followed. Especially notable were the works of the U.S. Lutheran/Roman Catholic Consultation., such as *Peter in the New Testament* (1973) and *Papal Primacy and the Universal Church* (1974). These bilateral documents on papal authority drew upon a concept described in the 1970s by James M. Robinson and Helmut Koester regarding "trajectories" through the early Christian period. Their concept argued that a notion implicitly and hesitantly present in the New Testament legitimately developed according to trajectories. A prime example was the development of Petrine ministry.

This interest in Petrine ministry has recently been further developed by John R. Quinn, archbishop emeritus of San Francisco, in *The*

Reform of the Papacy: The Costly Call to Christian Unity (1999), featured as part of Herder & Herder's new series *Ut Unum Sint*. Not all the recent works on the papacy possess Quinn's patient and tolerant tone, as is clear by contrasting his work to that of Gary Wills's *Papal Sin: Structures of Deceit* (2000).

2. Trinity and Christology: Apart from ecclesiology, a second area in systematic theology that has received special attention since 1965 has been, not surprisingly, the question of God, treatises on Trinity and Christology. In Christology this emphasis was preceded by a number of studies on the Jesus of the New Testament. One can point, for example, to the impact of the works by Raymond Brown and John P. Meier. The highly publicized and controversial positions often taken by members of the Jesus Seminar served as a wake-up call for others to relate the New Testament material to the experience of the early church to the Christology of Chalcedon.

One of the pioneering works in Christology, *The Reality of Jesus: An Essay in Christology* (1975), I am happy to note, was published by a theologian long associated with St. Michael's College: Professor Dermot A. Lane. This work written in an easily accessible style is also masterful in its pedagogy. It has had, at least among English-language readers, an even wider audience than Edward Schillebeeckx's *Jesus* (1979) and *Christ* (1980). What seems to be the overarching question of these christological studies is the status of the resurrection of Jesus and its relation to Christology. Two more recent volumes plea for deconstruction of Chalcedonian Christology: John Dominic Crossan's *The Historical Jesus: The Life of a Mediterranean Jewish Peasant* (1991) and Roger Haight's *Jesus, Symbol of God* (1999). Reviews of Haight are still coming in, but I note especially Dermot Lane's favorable review in the June 2000 issue of *Theological Studies*.

In trinitarian theology I would single out in the post–Vatican II era four works, all profound reflections on the core of trinitarian belief: Walter Kasper, *The God of Jesus Christ* (1984), Edmund Hill, O.P., *The Mystery of the Trinity* (1985), Catherine Mowry LaCugna, *God for Us: The Trinity and Christian Life* (1991), and David Coffey, *Deus Trinitas: The Doctrine of the Triune God* (1999). One of the many features that binds the four works together is their commitment to economical trinitarian theology and an attempt to update the classical formulations.

3. Eucharist. Here again the amount of publication by Catholics is notable. If one were to single out the more important works of historical theology of the Eucharist, one should cite the posthumous work of Edward J. Kilmartin, S.J., *The Eucharist in the West: History and Theology* (1998); Gary Macy's two monographs on the Eucharist, especially in the Middle Ages: *The Banquet's Wisdom* (1992), and *Treasures from the Storeroom: Medieval Religion and the Eucharist* (1999); and two works of Irish theologian David Noel Power: *The Sacrifice We Offer: Tridentine Dogma and Its Reinterpretation* (1987) and *The Eucharistic Mystery: Revitalizing the Tradition* (1992). These studies illustrate that there is sometimes a lag between what the liturgical scholars have established and the themes and views of some curial and even papal documents on the Eucharist.

4. Some new developing interests. As we advance further into the first decade of the twenty-first century, I expect ecumenical dialogue to be more and more overtaken by the dialogue with the other world religions, or *living faiths,* to use the terminology of the World Council of Churches. Vatican concerns about the uniqueness of Christ and the salvific role of other religions explain in part its call upon Jacques Dupuis to justify various formulations in his *Toward a Christian Theology of Religious Pluralism* (1997). We are only at the beginning of far-reaching theological discussion by Catholics regarding evangelization and the salvation of the nations.

As editor of *Theological Studies* I am often amazed at the number of articles submitted on Hans Urs von Balthasar. Not all of these studies are laudatory of the Swiss theologian. Some criticize his apparent lack of social concern. Balthasar is no longer simply the darling of the neo-conservatives who appeal to him in order to dethrone Karl Rahner from his hegemony.

Growing interest in Hispanic/Latino theology is occurring, though the size of this theological community in the United States is relatively small. Catholic African-Americans are seen to be speaking collectively and inviting the rest of the American Catholics to include their experience in our reflections. For this challenge by the African-American community I recommend the illuminating study *Taking Down Our Harps: Black Catholics in the United States*, edited by Diana L. Hayes and Cyprian Davis (1998).

Finally, I expect that theology will continue to be enriched by further attention to environmental theology, or ecology, beyond the pioneering work of Thomas M. Berry as outlined in such works as *Befriending the Earth: A Theology of Reconciliation Between Humans and the Earth* (1991).

CONCLUSION

If I have seemed harsh on the Vatican and all too easy on the American Catholic theological community, that is not my intention. The theological community in our country is in some disarray. It is not effectively communicating to the church at large. Theologians are devoting a disproportionate amount of time to undergraduate teaching—often to unwilling students—and are neglecting research, graduate education, production of *haute vulgarisation* that could be accessible to the wider Catholic community. We have not found a way yet of common discourse between the so-called conservative and progressive wings of our communities, our parishes, our Catholic newspapers, our publishing houses. We need to draw up various strategies. Programs such as St. Michael's will continue to be strong voices and contributors to our unfinished task.

NOTES

1. Karl Rahner, *Faith in a Wintry Season*, trans. and ed. Harvey Egan (New York: Crossroad, 1900).

2. See also Richard McCormick, "Punishing Dissent: Corralling Theologians, Containing Bishops," *Commonweal* 125/14 (August 14, 1998), 12–13.

3. See Francis A. Sullivan, *Magisterium: Teaching Authority in the Catholic Church* (New York: Paulist Press, 1983); and idem, *Creative Fidelity: Weighing and Interpreting Documents of the Magisterium* (New York: Paulist Press, 1996).

4. Francis Schüssler Fiorenza and John Galvin, eds., *Systematic Theology: Roman Catholic Perspectives*, 2 vols. (Minneapolis, Minn.: Fortress Press, 1991); Bernard Lauret and François Refoulé, eds., *Initiation à la pratique de la théologie*, 5 vols. (Paris: Cerf, 1982–83).

5. Joseph A. Komonchak, Mary Collins, and Dermot A. Lane, eds., *The New Dictionary of Theology* (Wilmington, Del.: Glazier, 1987); Peter E. Fink,

ed., *The New Dictionary of Sacramental Worship* (Collegeville, Minn.: Liturgical Press, 1990); Michael Downey, ed., *The New Dictionary of Catholic Spirituality* (Collegeville, Minn.: Liturgical Press, 1993); and Richard McBrien, ed., *HarperCollins Encyclopedia of Catholicism*, (San Francisco: HarperCollins, 1995).

 6. The English translation is *Church of Churches: The Ecclesiology of Communion*, trans. R. C. De Peaux (Collegeville, Minn.: Liturgical Press, 1992).

5. Catholic Moral Theology from 1960 to 2040: Accomplishments and Challenges for the Future

Philip S. Keane

I want to begin by expressing my gratitude to Edward Mahoney for inviting me to write this chapter. In a much deeper sense, I want to express my thanks to St. Michael's for having given me the opportunity to teach there in so many summer sessions over the past twenty some years. My gratitude extends especially to Fr. Paul Couture, S.S.E., without whose indefatigable energy this program would not exist, and to Betty Rafoul, whom we all miss so much during this time of celebration. But my thanks also goes to everyone associated with the graduate theology program: the wonderful students I have taught, the outstanding faculty members, and the administration and support personnel who have made everything here work so outstandingly well. St. Michael's has a special place in my heart, reaching back to those days in the early 1960s when my brother was an undergraduate here.

The task of this chapter is to present an assessment of what has happened in Catholic moral theology in the past forty years and also an assessment of what I think needs to happen in moral theology during the next forty years. Coincidentally, the early 1960s, when the graduate theology program began, is a very good time from which to begin such a task. The year 1960 effectively marked the end of the preconciliar manualist tradition. Hence, by beginning with 1960, I will be able to reflect on the entire conciliar and post-conciliar period in Catholic moral theology, noting both the many positive accomplishments of the past forty years and setting forth the agenda that I see for the first forty years of the twenty-first century. My approach in what follows is to describe nine major accomplishments of Catholic moral theology since 1960 and then to describe eleven issues that I think will need substantial attention and development during the next forty years. It is not my view that the eleven issues I highlight for the years ahead have been void of accomplishment since 1960, but I do believe that, in spite of some accomplishments, much remains to be done about these issues.

I confess at the outset that my choice of the twenty issues to be presented as either accomplishments or challenges may be a bit idiosyncratic. Any theologian has special areas of interest and accomplishment; these interests may well influence which issues are selected for this sort of reflective presentation and which are not. Others have certain areas of expertise, such as professional ethics and the ethics of genetic research, that range beyond my own special areas of interest. I trust that such scholars will balance out my idiosyncrasies.

First, let us turn to the major accomplishments of Catholic moral theology since 1960. The first accomplishment has been the development of a *historically conscious* approach in Catholic moral theology.[1] Before the 1960s moral theology was almost universally viewed in terms of fixed and changeless essences. All moral decisions were understood as logical deductions from moral principles. There was no need to study history, because nothing new ever really happened. As long as one knew the principles, the right answer was certain. Frequently, this earlier perspective was described as the classicist worldview. With some prehistory, but beginning especially in the 1960s, all of this changed dramatically. Serious Catholic scholarship in moral theology began to be seen as fundamentally incomplete if it did not include a historical-developmentalist approach. One of the important early examples of the historically conscious approach was the major study of contraception written by John Noonan in 1965.[2] The works of Charles Curran, throughout his distinguished career, have been very rich in the use of a historical methodology. This began in Curran's early books, but it can also be seen in the recent years, especially in works such as Curran's study of the earlier American moralists Thomas Boquillon, Aloysius Sabetti, and John B. Hogan.[3]

Personally, I find that the use of a historically conscious approach makes moral theology much more dynamic, real, and alive. I do not mean by this to imply that the earlier manualist tradition was all bad.

Indeed, I have become a collector of the earlier manuals and frequently refer to them. But surely the use of the historically conscious methodology has been one of the great accomplishments of Catholic moral theology in the past forty years.

The second of the main accomplishments of Catholic moral theology since 1960 has been the way in which moral theology has integrated the major renewals of Catholic Thomistic philosophy that took place in the twentieth century. I say "renewals" in the plural because there were actually two major streams of twentieth-century renewal in Catholic philosophy. The earlier stream, associated with scholars such as Jacques Maritain and Étienne Gilson, was able to integrate Catholic philosophy and insights from modern existentialist thought.[4] The pastoral and personalist thrust in today's moral theology owes much to this first stream of philosophical renewal. We will discuss these pastoral and personalist developments later.

The second and even more significant stream of philosophical renewal can be seen in the works of scholars such as Joseph Maréchal, Bernard Lonergan, and Karl Rahner.[5] Earlier forms of Thomism had focused almost exclusively on the realities that human persons are able to know. But Maréchal, Lonergan, and Rahner—known as transcendental Thomists—also focused on us as creative human knowers, arguing that our foundational ability to learn is as important as what we learn. From this insight a rich and much more dynamic philosophy of ourselves as developing human persons came into being. Many moralists of the recent past have helped integrate the insights of the transcendental Thomists into a much more integrated and holistic approach to moral theology. I think, for instance, of the German scholar Josef Fuchs, particularly his famous article on the absoluteness of moral terms.[6] Fuchs is an interesting case because his earliest works, from the 1950s and early 1960s, are clearly of a piece with the classic manualist tradition. But the later 1960s saw a significant change in Fuchs's approach. One can almost tell when he began to read Rahner and the others in depth.

The third main accomplishment, stemming from the first and second, has been the development of what I might call an enlightened natural-law methodology. Such a methodology does not imply any denial of the heart of the natural-law tradition or any loss of confidence about the key natural-law insights on universal moral norms and on the goodness of human persons and human society. But modern natural-law methodology focuses not only on moral principles but on us as creative and reflective knowers of the difference between right and wrong. The physicalisms of the past, in which morality often focused too exclusively on sexuality, are thus avoided. Also, in light of historical complexity, the temptation to think that all the answers are clear and simple is set aside. But none of this means that modern natural-law thinkers are abandoning the idea that human persons are able to come to clear moral insights and principles.

The impetus to this sort of revitalized natural-law approach actually began in the 1930s with the pioneering work of Dom Lottin.[7] But the last forty years have seen much helpful work on this theme. In the United States, I think of the work of scholars such as Charles Curran and Richard McCormick.[8] European names that come to mind include Josef Fuchs, Bruno Schüller, Gerard Hughes, John Mahoney, and Franz Böckle.[9] Not all of these scholars are exactly the same, but they all connect to the revitalization of natural law. Another point to be made before moving on is this: For all its importance and coherence as a tradition, I think that the natural-law tradition needs to be open to other ways of construing the moral life. Many modern Catholic scholars, without abandoning natural law, sense a need to explore some other directions for the future.

The fourth major accomplishment of Catholic moral theology has been the development of a much stronger sense of pastoral sensitivity to the real issues faced by real people. At one level such sensitivity has been a longstanding part of the Roman Catholic tradition, beginning with Saint Thomas; it has been especially noted since the time of Saint Alphonsus Liguori, the eighteenth-century founder of the Redemptorists, who is usually called the father of modern moral theology. In the middle of the twentieth century, however, the key themes of the pastoral sensitivity tradition—that we need to pay attention to the complexities of human understanding and freedom—were taken largely for granted. It was assumed that understanding and freedom were simple issues, so that those who did something wrong were more or less automatically fully responsible for what they had done. Who needed to ask any pastoral questions?

But in the past four or five decades—inspired by modern personalist thinkers and by the developments in Catholic philosophy and historical thinking—Catholic moral theology has become much more pastoral.

This has shown itself especially in the revitalized understanding of sin that came from the fundamental-option theory, which is well accepted today even if it needs some important nuances. Even magisterial statements have joined in the trend of noting the pastoral care necessary in the assessment of moral responsibility.[10]

When I think of this whole achievement of a more pastorally sensitive Catholic moral theology, I think especially of the great Redemptorist theologian Bernard Häring. Häring once taught in the St. Michael's program, and if one looks at his second three-volume work, *Free and Faithful in Christ,* one can find the names of some St. Michael's students who assisted him with the details of the trilogy.[11] For the record, while there are a number of worthy candidates, I consider Häring to be the single most important Catholic moral theologian of the twentieth century. When we think about the changed spirit of Catholic moral theology since Vatican II, Häring had more impact on that change than any other scholar.[12] The agenda he set for us has not been completed, so I will be returning to Häring in the section on future challenges for moral theology.

The fifth major accomplishment of moral theology since the 1960s is that it has become so much more ecumenical. In the United States this movement toward moral ecumenism actually had roots even earlier, for instance, in the use of a natural-law methodology by John Coleman Bennett in the 1940s and in Bennett's references in the 1950s to the writings of John Courtney Murray.[13] Today, ecumenism in moral theology is taken almost for granted, especially in the field of social ethics. I regularly find myself assigning students to read the two Niebuhrs, Bennett, Brunner, Ramsey, Gustafson, Hauerwas, and a number of others.[14] I myself have received a great deal of insight from my extended reading of Reinhold Niebuhr. After Rahner, Reinhold Niebuhr may well be the most important intellectual influence on my thinking. All this is very refreshing and dramatically different from Catholic moral theology in the middle of the twentieth century, when Protestant writers were largely ignored.

The sixth major accomplishment of Catholic moral theology since 1960 has to do with the changing face of who does moral theology. In the manualist period the understanding was that moral theology was to be done exclusively by priests, and the primary purpose of moral theology was understood to be to help candidates for the priesthood prepare to hear confessions. This approach, which was still the norm when I entered the seminary, harked back to the Irish church and its development of the Penetentials in the second half of the first millennium after Christ. Yes, there are still some priests who work in moral theology. But increasingly in the past forty years Catholic religious and Catholic laypeople have become esteemed scholars of moral theology. Of special note are today's Catholic moral theologians who are women. Names such as Margaret Farley, Lisa Cahill, Anne Patrick, Christine Gudorf, Jean Porter, and Barbara Andolsen quickly come to mind.[15] Their work has enriched and broadened the discipline of moral theology in a great many ways. One result is that even the traditional types of moral theologians (like me) approach the discipline quite differently than was the case in the past. Not all of these women moral theologians make use of the same methodologies, but the mention of them surely reminds us of the importance of feminism in today's moral theology.

Before moving to my seventh through ninth contemporary accomplishments of Catholic moral theology, let me note that the six accomplishments so far mentioned all address matters related to the fundamental structure of Catholic moral theology. The final three accomplishments speak to three specific areas of Catholic moral theology: sexual ethics, health-care ethics, and social justice.

And so we turn to the seventh accomplishment, which has to do with sexual ethics. I think the great accomplishment since 1960 is that the personalism which has marked much of modern Catholic moral theology has led to the development of a holistic theological anthropology of human sexuality, to a vision in which sexuality is understood as a fundamental constituent of human personality instead of as a series of discrete actions. This has led to a much richer theology of marriage as a covenantal relationship between two persons, a theme foreshadowed as far back as the work of Dr. Hubert Doms in the late 1930s.[16] It has also led us to focus on a whole host of new questions in the area of sexual ethics, perhaps most notably on the need for gender justice, that is, genuinely nondiscriminatory relationships between the sexes. I highlight this broader theological anthropology of sexuality because I think it is fair to say that all serious Catholic theology now supports this vision. It can clearly be found in the teachings of the magisterium.[17] Of course, there continues to be much debate about the implications of this anthropology in terms of how moral principles apply to specific sexual behaviors. We will return to this debate later when we reflect on the agenda of moral theology in the years ahead.

The eighth area of accomplishment in Catholic moral theology in the post–Vatican II era has to do with the unprecedented developments in medical science in the past several decades. Medicine has progressed to the point that it can now bring people back from the very edge of death through the use of CPR and other modern techniques. But when is it right to use these techniques, and when is it better not to use them? Many doctors and hospitals have been so schooled in the milieu of modern science that they can all too easily think that today's life-extending techniques should always be put into use. Catholicism, in facing these issues, has the very distinct advantage of having a five-hundred-year-old tradition that holds that, while life is sacred, death is part of the human story, so there should be prudent limits on just how far we should go in prolonging human life, especially when death is clearly close at hand.[18] Catholicism has a deep affinity for the old French proverb, prominently associated with Dr. Trudeau and his work on tuberculosis a century ago: "Sometimes to cure, often to relieve pain, always to give care and comfort." Working from this background, Catholicism has emerged as a highly significant dialogue partner in today's discussions about the ethics of care for the dying. Very many doctors and hospitals and even governmental agencies have been able to establish better policies on care of the dying, in no small part because of the impact of the Roman Catholic moral tradition. It is impossible not to mention again the name of Richard McCormick in this context, but other scholars such as John Paris, Richard Sparks, Ron Hamel, and Jim Keenan have also been important contributors to the recent Catholic approach to ethics at the end of human life.[19]

My ninth and last theme on the accomplishment side of the ledger has to do with the enormously significant developments in Catholic social teaching during the past forty years. Modern Catholic social teaching began much earlier with the work of Pope Leo XIII in the 1890s. But in the past four decades some very special things have happened in Catholic social teaching. Catholic economic theory has become much more even-handed in its criticism of both capitalist and socialist economic systems. This can be seen in the encyclicals of both Pope John XXIII, with his famous comments on socialization, and Pope John Paul II, particularly in *Sollicitudo rei socialis*.[20] It can be seen as well in

the U.S. bishops' famous 1986 pastoral letter *Economic Justice for All.*
Catholicism has also taken on a pivotally important role in questions of
peace and nuclear disarmament, with the U.S. Catholic bishops having
played a major role on this issue.[21] Newer social issues have been raised
to the surface in Catholic social thought, including environmental or
ecological ethics, international debt reduction, and capital punishment.
For the record, John Paul II has been far more outspoken against capital
punishment than any of his predecessors, even causing the *Catechism
of the Catholic Church* to be revised to reflect his growing opposition to
capital punishment.[22] When all these themes are considered, it is clear
that the recent decades have been a time of enormous, even spectacular
progress in Catholic social teaching.

These comments conclude my summary of nine major areas of
development in Catholic moral theology since 1960. In presenting these
areas, I am hardly claiming that everything possible has already been
done in any of these nine areas. All of them are open to and in need of
further development. Nonetheless, the case is clear that moral theology
has achieved much in these areas. For this we should be refreshed and
thankful.

I now turn to some areas in which there are clear needs for future
development in Catholic moral theology. There are some connections to
the areas of accomplishment that I am sure that you will notice. But any
one-for-one parallel would be forced and artificial, so I present eleven
areas of needed development.

First, I think Catholic moral theology still faces the challenge of
becoming much more biblically based. No doubt some of you are surprised that I list the topic of moral theology and the scriptures as a challenge rather than an accomplishment. After all, the call to be more
biblical was one of the key agenda items of Vatican II in regard to moral
theology.[23] It is true that there have been some important successes in
terms of a more scripturally based moral theology. Bernard Häring,
whom I mentioned earlier, was outstanding for his ability to imbue his
entire approach to moral theology with a biblical spirit. I have a number
of colleagues who have effectively taught college or graduate courses
on scripture and moral theology. But on the whole, my opinion is that
the response to Vatican II's call for a more biblically grounded moral
theology has been somewhat disappointing. I think the basic issue is
this: Catholic moral theology has spent so many centuries relying on

natural law and not making much use of scripture that it will take quite a long time for a biblical spirit to become an intrinsic part of the fiber of Catholic moral thinking. Recall, for example, that such a classic twentieth-century moral text as John A. Ryan's *Distributive Justice* (1916) only cited scripture three times in over five hundred pages and then only quite coincidentally.[24] It takes a long time to move beyond deeply ingrained approaches such as this, and there is clearly much unfinished in terms of the building of a genuinely biblical Catholic moral theology.

Second, Catholic moral theology still has much to do to understand itself as being not only about individual decisions but also about the conversion of the human heart and the human mind so that we become good moral persons, not only makers of good decisions. To say this in another way, moral theology has before it the task of uniting the moral and the spiritual life into an integrated whole. The call to holiness and the call to decision-making cannot be seen as separate entities; they are interactive parts of one process. Classic Catholic thought was aware of this theme, especially in terms of Saint Thomas's stress on the life of virtue. But for much of twentieth-century Catholicism, prayer and the spiritual life became something for the chapel, and action became something for the marketplace, with little interaction between the life of prayer and the life of the marketplace.[25] While I do not agree with all the elements of his approach, I must congratulate the contemporary Protestant scholar Stanley Hauerwas for retrieving the Thomistic tradition of virtue and character development in a way that many Catholics have failed to do.[26] To be fair, there are notable Catholic successes on this topic of the union of the moral and spiritual life, including some of Rich Gula's recent work on themes such as spirituality and discernment.[27] But I must still argue that there is much unfinished in terms of the integration of moral and spiritual theology.

Third, let me speak about philosophy. Above I praised Catholic moral theology for its open dialogue with twentieth-century Thomism. But there are many important philosophical systems flourishing today. I think that a major task for moral theology in the new millennium will be to expand its philosophical dialogue partners and become more conversant with a whole range of philosophical systems. More and more people, Catholics and others, are being educated in broad streams of philosophical diversity. How can moral theology be effective if it does not understand the real needs and interests of people? And how can it understand these needs without opening itself more fully to the rich variety of philosophical reflection that is part of today's world? I do not mean to imply that none of this has happened in the past, for it surely has happened in great recent figures like Rahner and Lonergan.[28] But so much more is necessary here. I also do not mean to imply that the need for broader philosophical dialogue means that Thomism is in trouble. Indeed, if Thomism, the church's *philosophia perennis,* is as good as the church thinks it is (and I think it is), one can only assume that Thomism will emerge even stronger from the philosophical dialogue that is so much needed in these times.

The fourth area calling out for future work by moral theology has to do with the almost indescribably remarkable progress that science is making as the millennium begins. In this context one quickly thinks about the human genome project, about cloning, and about the whole field of the genetic sciences. But there are many other important areas in which science is moving forward very rapidly. In the future, in order to speak credibly on a wide variety of issues, moral theology will need to be fully conversant with the scientific understandings that are part of these issues. Only intense ongoing dialogue between moral theology and the sciences will make this kind of credibility possible for moral theology of the future.[29] An important consequence of this dialogue is that individual moral theologians will need to concentrate on specific areas within science. The traditional idea of the generalist moral theologian who knew something about every moral issue will very likely be impossible in the future. Instead, individual moral theologians will have expertise in specific moral/scientific areas but not in every area. I think, for instance, that I am more conversant with health-care economics than Edward Mahoney, but he certainly knows more than I about ethics and genetics. In this context it might also help to recall that when Richard McCormick ended his twenty years as the author of "Notes on Moral Theology," *Theological Studies* had to put together a team of four scholars to replace him.[30] The growing need for scientific knowledge may have made McCormick the last universalist moral theologian whom any of us will remember.

Here I want to note a fifth area of the future agenda for moral theology, an area related to the sciences but having a more specific focus. I refer to the awesome progress of computer science and information technology. My question here is this: What will it mean for young people to have so much of their learning experience computer based? Christianity is profoundly a religion of belief in the power of God's word, with that word being largely mediated to us through the words of the artist, the poet, the musician, and the dancer. In the past people have responded to the word of God because they have heard laughter, sensed the comic, felt—and deeply felt—the tragic. Will persons whose learning experience is strongly computer based really be able to *hear* the word of God?[31] Will they hear the word when it is preached? Will they listen to their prophets? Will they be able to have a dream as Martin Luther King Jr. did? Or will the technological bent of their learning make words mere utilitarian devices, so that the sense of poetry disappears? If words do become mere exercises of utility, will moral community still be possible? Some of my own most important past writing has been on the importance of moral imagination as a crucial element in the formation of moral insight and moral community.[32] In the years ahead I think it will be critically important for moral theology—and indeed for all of theology—to reflect deeply on this question of how moral sensitivity will be able to be developed in the computer age. I am certainly not speaking against modern computer technologies, but we simply must ask just what impact these technologies are having on our development as human persons, as moral persons.

My sixth area for future activity in moral theology has to do with the need to expand from an ecumenical perspective to an interfaith perspective. Some of this has already happened, especially in the case of dialogue with Judaism. But much more dialogue with all of the world's great religions would be helpful. I acknowledge that dialogues with some of the other traditions will be different because we will not be working from a common set of scriptures. Sometimes the dialogue will need to focus on the cultural context of other religions as much as on their specific theological insights into the meaning of God. In some respects the dialogue with the other great religions may never have as much specific focus as the dialogues within Christianity or even as Jewish/Christian dialogue. But such broader dialogues are very necessary, and they relate strongly to the possibilities of global peace and justice in the forthcoming century. My hope is that, when they find it appropriate, Catholic moral theologians of the new century will be as ready to assign readings from the other religions as Catholic moralists have been ready to assign readings from other Christian communities during the past forty years.

The past several sections have all called for dialogue as an essential element for the future of moral theology—dialogue with philosophy, with the sciences, and with other faith traditions. Here, as my seventh future agenda item, I want to call for an even broader sort of dialogue as a crucial challenge for the future of moral theology. We live in a rapidly changing world, a world in which people of many languages and cultures are living in closer and closer contact with one another. This change has a special impact on Roman Catholicism with its worldwide presence. In view of all this, I think that moral theology of the future will have to develop a broadly multicultural base.[33] Otherwise, how will the church's moral tradition be shared with all the peoples of the world? How will the mutual learning and understanding that are necessary for adequate moral judgment take place? Hence, beyond the specific dialogues I have already mentioned, the moral theology of the new century will need to engage in an ongoing multicultural dialogue, so that moral theology can truly relate to the peoples of Africa, Asia, the Americas, and a host of other places, as well as retaining its historical and largely European roots.

The eighth area of future agenda for moral theology flows from some of the accomplishments we discussed earlier, from the development of a modern Thomist philosophical outlook, from the revitalization of natural law, and from the articulation of a holistic sexual anthropology. Based on these developments a number of significant Catholic moral theologians have developed an important new approach to the meaning and character of concrete moral norms. In this context one thinks about the work of European scholars such as Josef Fuchs, Bruno Schüller, and Louis Janssens.[34] In the United States, Richard McCormick contributed enormously to this understanding of moral norms, especially in his monograph, *Ambiguity in Moral Choice*.[35] Rich Gula has also made important contributions to the research on moral norms with his call for a revisionist approach to moral theology.[36]

What needs to be said next is that, in spite of all this important scholarship, very substantial segments of the Catholic moral community, including the magisterium, have not accepted the approach to concrete moral norms that has been developed by McCormick and the others.[37] Please note that I am speaking about concrete moral norms, because there is a widespread Catholic consensus about the role and meaning of the more universal and fundamental moral norms. So my specific point is that there remains much tension in Catholic moral theology about the nature and application of concrete moral norms. This tension is felt in many areas in Catholic moral theology, but it is especially present in the area of sexual ethics. So further scholarship and dialogue on the nature and application of moral norms are clearly great necessities for Catholic moral theology in the years ahead. At this point I am not sure whether this dialogue will proceed best if it bases itself on the previous work of McCormick and others. Or would it perhaps be better to explore entirely new approaches that might get us beyond some of the tensions of the recent past? I am certain of this: Catholic moral theology will benefit greatly if it can find suitable ways to overcome the recent tensions about concrete moral norms.

The mention of this tension about concrete moral norms creates a natural context from which to raise the ninth of my future agenda items for Catholic moral theology. This agenda item has to do with the relationship between moral theology and the church's magisterium or teaching office. Because the magisterium has not been open to some of the aspects of the scholarship on moral norms that I just cited, it is surely clear that there has been some tension between the magisterium and some moral theologians over the past twenty years or so. I do think that this tension is very often overstated, especially in the popular media, which likes to promote controversy. And I could certainly cite many examples of important cooperation between moral theologians and the magisterium. But even with these careful qualifications, who can deny that the tensions exist?

Surely everyone recognizes the role of the magisterium and its need to articulate Catholic teaching clearly. Everyone also recognizes the place of moral theology, with its task of probing, searching more deeply, and seeking to find ways of articulating Catholic moral teaching more appropriately in changing historical circumstances. Indeed, in the end, it would not be possible for the magisterium to accomplish its primary teaching task were it not for the service given to the church by its theologians, both in moral theology and in other fields. What is needed, therefore, is not some sort of either/or confrontation between theologians and the magisterium but a model in which the roles of both the magisterium and the theologians can be respected and supported. I think it fair to say that in the recent past the church community as a whole has not done as well as might be desired in working out a fully suitable relationship between moral theology and the magisterium. It is very much to be desired that all of us find ways to do better with this issue in the years and decades ahead.

I have one last point to make on this issue of moral theology and the magisterium. If we fail to make the progress for which I am calling here, it is hard not to worry about whether the church will have enough moral theologians in the next generation, at least moral theologians who are part of Catholic-sponsored institutions such as colleges and seminaries. Might the tension I have described discourage gifted young people from taking up careers in moral theology? No one can say for sure, but I think the question is fair. Personally, I hope to have a number of productive years ahead of me, but the invitation to be a principal speaker at a retrospective event such as this cannot help but make me reflect that the shadows are lengthening, that I have far fewer scholarly years left than those I have already spent. So it is natural to wonder about who will come along next in moral theology.

When I listed the accomplishments of Catholic moral theology, I ended with comments on the three specific areas of sexual ethics, health-care ethics, and social justice. I think the past two sections about concrete norms and the magisterium have had enough allusions to sexual ethics, so I have only two more areas of challenge to describe: health-care ethics and social justice.

The tenth area of challenge for the future has to do with health-care ethics. I mentioned earlier that Catholic moral thought has made outstanding contributions to the development of clinical medical ethics over the recent decades. But today there are important new challenges in health-care ethics in addition to the need for reflection on the scientific advances I referred to above. First of all profit-making entities control many aspects of health-care delivery today; thus it is harder and harder for religious providers of health care to maintain their integrity and avoid getting sucked into the management tactics used by the for-profit health-care companies. To say this in another way, organizational ethics are very much needed in today's health-care systems, and I believe Catholic moral theology has an important challenge to help the caregivers find ways to make their delivery systems function in a ethically appropriate manner, a manner that respects the dignity of both the patients and the employees.[38]

Beyond this question of striving for systems of health delivery that are in themselves more justly organized and managed, there is the mega-question about health care and distributive justice. There are now 44.3 million persons in the United States who lack any health insurance.[39] The World Health Organization recently published a study which argues that, for all the wealth of the United States, thirty six countries have better and more just health systems than does the United States.[40] If we shift our perspective to a global basis and consider that there are several countries in the world where life expectancy is as low as the mid to late thirties, the question about health-care justice becomes even deeper.[41] I see it as pivotally important for moral theology to use its insights, in conjunction with others, to embark on programs of strong and active advocacy for justice in health-care delivery. I think it can be argued that the good of health care is a central enough human good that the peace and stability of future generations truly depend on the achievement of global justice in health care. I very much hope that this new century does not see the terrible wars of the twentieth century. As I see it, just health care is one of the keys to world peace.

My eleventh and final area of challenge builds on the justice issues to which I have just referred. I stated earlier that I think Catholic social teaching has had some outstanding accomplishments in the latter decades of the twentieth century. But I still see one large problem here. I think that there are too many Catholics who do not take the church's social teaching seriously, who think that the real moral concerns of the church are about sexuality and medicine, and that therefore we do not really have to pay attention to the social teachings of the church. No one need apologize for having moral concerns about sexuality and medicine. But these issues are simply not the whole of the Catholic moral agenda. Hence, I think that in the coming decades Catholic moral theology faces the pressing task of finding ways to articulate the church's social teachings with such force and clarity that all Catholics begin to take these teachings with the seriousness that they deserve now and have deserved since the 1890s. As I said in the last section, the peace and tranquility of the entire world will depend in part on a more genuine and wholehearted acceptance of these teachings.

And so ends my assessment of the great achievements of Catholic moral theology since the St. Michael's graduate theology program began in 1960 and my assessment of the many daunting challenges that will face moral theology in the next forty years. I hope I have shown how much has been accomplished and also how much remains to be done. I thought about trying to offer some integrating remarks at the end, but I hope what I said is reasonably clear.

I do have one closing comment. The former students who are here all know about my deep and abiding fondness for the wonderful mountains that rise so prominently on both sides of Lake Champlain. Many of the students have accompanied me on the treks up Camel's Hump that have always been a part of my summer teaching here. Many also know of my love for Genesis 49, which speaks of a God who is far beyond these mountains, who is, in the words of the Vulgate, "the desire of the everlasting hills." I know that I have held out some hard future agenda this morning. If we can have the courage and the faith to believe in our God, who both loves us personally and whose eternity goes beyond the hills of space and time, then I am filled with hope that we can continue the journey and keep meeting the agenda, no matter how daunting it may get. My prayer is that this is exactly what will happen. And my prayer—and my love—is for St. Michael's and for all of you.

NOTES

1. See Bernard Lonergan, "The Transition from a Classicist World-View to Historical-Mindedness," in *A Second Collection,* ed. William Ryan and Bernard Tyrrell (Philadelphia: Westminster Press, 1974), 1–10.

2. John T. Noonan, *Contraception: A History of Its Treatment by the Catholic Theologians and Canonists* (Cambridge, Mass.: Harvard University Press, 1965).

3. For an early example of Curran's use of history, see "Masturbation and Objectively Grave Matter," in *A New Look at Christian Morality* (Notre Dame, Ind.: Fides Press, 1968), 201–22. More recently, see *The Origins of Moral Theology in the United States: Three Different Approaches* (Washington, D.C.: Georgetown University Press, 1997).

4. See Donald and Idella Gallagher, eds. *A Maritain Reader* (Garden City, N.Y.: Doubleday, 1966); Anton C. Pegis, ed., *A Gilson Reader* (Garden City, N.Y.: Doubleday, 1957).

5. See Joseph Donceel, ed., *A Maréchal Reader* (New York: Herder and Herder, 1970); Bernard Lonergan, *Insight: A Study of Human Understanding* (London: Longmans, Green, 1957); Karl Rahner, *Spirit in the World* (New York: Herder and Herder, 1968).

6. Josef Fuchs, "The Absoluteness of Behavioral Moral Norms," in *Personal Responsibility and Christian Morality* (Washington, D.C.: Georgetown University Press, 1983), 115–52. For an example of the earlier Fuchs, see *Natural Law: A Theological Investigation* (New York: Sheed and Ward, 1965).

7. Odon Lottin, *Le Droit Naturel chez Thomas d'Aquin et ses prédécesseurs,* 2d. ed. (Bruges: Charles Beyart, 1931).

8. Charles Curran, "Natural Law in Contemporary Moral Theology," in *Contemporary Problems in Moral Theology* (Notre Dame, Ind.: Fides Press, 1970), 97–158; Richard McCormick, "The Natural Law: Recent Literature," in *Readings in Moral Theology No. 7: The Natural Law and Theology,* ed. Charles Curran and Richard McCormick (New York: Paulist Press, 1991), 173–83.

9. A contribution by each of these authors is included in Curran and McCormick, *Readings in Moral Theology No. 7.*

10. Congregation for the Doctrine of the Faith, "Declaration on Certain Questions Concerning Sexual Questions," (29 December 1975), no. 10 (in *Origins* 5 [1976], 490).

11. Bernard Häring, *Free and Faithful in Christ: Moral Theology for Clergy and Laity,* 3 vols. (New York: Seabury/Crossroad, 1978–81).

12. For Vatican II's key statement on the renewal of moral theology, see *Optatam Totius (Decree on Priestly Formation),* no. 16, in *The Documents of Vatican II,* ed. Walter Abbott (New York: America Press, 1966), 452.

13. John Coleman Bennett, *Christian Ethics and Social Policy* (New York: Charles Scribner's, 1946); idem, *Christians and the State* (New York: Charles Scribner's, 1958).

14. Among the fundamental works I use are Reinhold Niebuhr, *The Nature and Destiny of Man,* 2 vols. (Louisville, Ky.: Westminster/John Knox Press, 1996 [orig., 1941–43]); H. Richard Niebuhr, *Christ and Culture* (New York: Harper & Row, 1951 [orig., 1941–43]); Emil Brunner, *The Divine Imperative: A Study in Christian Ethics* (Philadelphia: Westminster Press, 1947); Paul Ramsey, *Deeds and Rules in Christian Ethics* (New York: Charles Scribner's Sons, 1967); James Gustafson, *Ethics in a Theocentric Context,* 2 vols. (Chicago: University of Chicago Press, 1981–84); Stanley Hauerwas, *Character and the Christian Life: A Study in Theological Ethics* (Notre Dame, Ind.: University of Notre Dame Press, 1994).

15. Works by these and other Catholic women in moral theology can be found in Charles Curran, Margaret Farley, and Richard McCormick, eds., *Readings in Moral Theology No. 9: Feminist Ethics and the Catholic Tradition* (New York: Paulist Press, 1996).

16. Dr. Hubert Doms, *The Meaning of Marriage* (New York: Sheed and Ward, 1939).

17. For an example of the magisterium's basic openness to key tenets of modern sexual anthropology, see Congregation for the Doctrine of the Faith, "Declaration on Certain Questions Concerning Sexual Questions," 485.

18. For a brief summary of the early history of the Catholic tradition on this issue, see Richard McCormick and John Paris, "The Catholic Tradition on the Use of Nutrition and Fluids," *America* 156 (1987), 358.

19. Samples of these scholars' works include John Paris, "The Catholic Tradition on the Use of Nutrition and Fluids," in *Birth, Suffering and Death: Catholic Perspectives at the Edges of Life,* ed. Kevin Wildes, et al. (Boston: Kluwer Academic Books, 1992), 189–208; Richard Sparks, *To Treat or Not to Treat? Bioethics and the Handicapped Newborn* (New York: Paulist Press, 1988); Ronald Hamel and Edwin DuBose, eds., *Must We Suffer Our Way to Death?: Cultural and Theological Perspectives on Death by Choice* (Dallas, Tex.: SMU Press, 1996); James Keenan, ed., *Catholic Ethicists on HIV/AIDS Prevention* (New York: Continuum Publishing Co., 2000).

20. For John XXIII on socialization, see *Mater et magistra,* nos. 59–67; for John Paul II's criticism of both capitalism and socialism, see *Sollicitudo rei socialis,* nos. 21–22.

21. See National Conference of Catholic Bishops, *The Challenge of Peace: God's Promise and Our Response* (1983); idem, *Economic Justice for All* (1986).

22. *Catechism of the Catholic Church* (Washington, D.C.: United States Catholic Conference, 1994).

23. See, for example, Häring, *Free and Faithful in Christ.*

24. John A. Ryan, *Distributive Justice* (New York: Macmillan, 1916).

25. For a classic statement of how our life and work can be supported by prayer, but how prayer cannot be enriched by life and work, see J-B Chautard, *The Soul of the Apostolate* (1920; reprint Rockford, Ill.: TAN Books, 1992).

26. Hauerwas, *Character and the Christian Life.*

27. Richard M. Gula, *Moral Discernment* (New York: Paulist Press, 1997); idem, *The Good Life: Where Morality and Spirituality Converge* (New York: Paulist Press, 1999).

28. Rahner had significant dialogues with German idealism and with Heideggerian existentialism. British empiricism was a key dialogue partner for Lonergan.

29. For a helpful study of this theme, see James M. Gustafson, *Intersections: Science, Theology, and Ethics* (Cleveland, Ohio: Pilgrim Press, 1996).

30. Richard McCormick, *Notes on Moral Theology 1965–1980* (Lanham, Md.: University Press of America, 1983); idem, *Notes on Moral Theology 1981–84* (Lanham, Md.: University Press of America, 1985).

31. This evokes Karl Rahner's famous work *Hearer of the Word: Laying the Foundation for a Philosophy of Religion* (1969; New York: Continuum Books, 1994).

32. Philip S. Keane, *Christian Ethics and Imagination* (New York: Paulist Press, 1984).

33. See William Cenkner, ed., *The Multicultural Church: A New Landscape in U.S. Theologies* (New York: Paulist Press, 1996).

34. Pertinent articles by each of these authors can be found in Charles Curran and Richard McCormick, eds., *Readings in Moral Theology No. 1: Moral Norms and Catholic Tradition* (New York: Paulist Press, 1979).

35. Richard McCormick, *Ambiguity in Moral Choice* (Milwaukee, Wis.: Marquette University Press, 1977).

36. Richard Gula, *Reason Informed by Faith: Foundations of Catholic Morality* (New York: Paulist Press, 1994).

37. For Pope John Paul II's concerns about this issue, see his encyclical *Veritatis splendor* (6 August 1993). While I tend to agree with the pope's basic concerns about moral norms, the positions of the various writers often have nuances and subtleties that are too complex for complete treatment, even in a lengthy encyclical.

38. For a helpful summary of the issues related to organizational ethics in health care, see Leonard J. Weber, "Taking on Organizational Ethics," *Health Progress* 78 (1997), 20–23, 32.

39. The figure of 44.3 million was the estimate of the Census Bureau in the second half of 1999.

40. Rosie Mestel, "Despite Big Spending, U.S. Ranks 37th in Study of Global Health Care," *Los Angeles Times* (21 June 2000).

41. According to the 2000 *Britannica Book of the Year* (Chicago: Encyclopaedia Britannica, 2000), life expectancy in Malawi is 35.9 years for men and 36.5 years for women (p. 653). In Zambia, life expectancy is 36.8 years for men and 37.3 years for women (p. 746). In Swaziland, life expectancy is 37.3 years for men and 39.8 years for women (p. 715). In Zimbabwe, life expectancy is 39.1 years for men and 39.2 years for women. Although traffic accidents and malaria continue to be enormous problems in these countries, it is the spread of AIDS that has significantly lowered life expectancy in recent years.

6. A Spirited Community Encounters Christ: Liturgical and Sacramental Theology and Practice

Kevin W. Irwin

INTRODUCTION

At the outset I would like to assert and presume that all liturgy is paschal, that all liturgy is pastoral, and that all liturgy is both a worthy object of theological reflection and a privileged means for the enactment of God's kingdom among us and the building up of the body of Christ on earth. Liturgy and sacraments always enact the paschal mystery. They are the church's central means of experiencing and taking part in Christ's dying and rising. Liturgy "accomplishes" this by the proclamation and enactment of the word of God, engagement in symbolic rites and gestures, most often accompanied by prayers that bless God and articulate what it is we believe about God and what we believe to be happening in liturgy, through the use of the arts (especially music and architecture), which reflects the genius of humanity's artistic abilities offered to God in acts of doxology.[1]

Liturgy and sacraments are also always pastoral in that they are enacted in specific contexts of church communities and have an impact on the faith life of those communities. Liturgy can legitimately be regarded as pastoral theology, because it is a reflection on what has occurred in the act of liturgy in varied church settings and on the theological meanings inherent in the liturgy as enacted. Therefore, I want to distinguish this kind of pastoral theology from the common assumption that "pastoral" means suggestions for planning and celebrating the reformed liturgy.[2]

On the one hand, the study of liturgy is a true theological science and as such is worthy of the effort to determine its precise scope, tasks, and method. Yet it is also a privileged means for experiencing and enacting God's kingdom among us for the building up of the church.[3] This is to suggest that liturgy is both an end in itself in terms of an academic study as well as a means to enacting the paschal mystery among us. Keeping this distinction in mind can help frame much of what I want to raise for discussion. Concretely this means that liturgy is both a true theological *locus* and, as such, an object of study. It is also a central means for deepening conversion to Christ, personal sanctification, church unity, and an ever more vibrant witnessing before the world of what we believe. The adage *lex orandi, lex credendi* will be operative throughout all that follows.

The purpose of this chapter is to invite conversation on the range of issues related to both the study and the pastoral implementation of liturgy and sacraments over the last four decades. Specific examples from liturgies and sacraments are meant to be simply that, examples, and are not meant to be exhaustive. The following is divided into four parts, dealing with (1) liturgical-sacramental method: an ongoing task, (2) liturgical reform: implemented and unfinished, (3) liturgical and sacramental rhetoric and reality, and (4) confidence in the liturgy.

1. LITURGICAL-SACRAMENTAL METHOD: AN ONGOING TASK

In a sense the twentieth century can be regarded as *the* century of liturgical method in the Western church; it has been a unique period for developing the study of what is sometimes termed *liturgics* or *liturgiology* and for delineating what constitutes method in liturgical studies today. The statement in the *Constitution on the Sacred Liturgy (Sacrosanctum concilium)* that the liturgy ought to be studied under its theological, historical, spiritual, pastoral, and juridical aspects (no. 16) simply reiterated what had been occurring since the end of the nineteenth century (at least in some circles)—an integral study of the liturgy in its many aspects, not just its external performance (rubrics). Indisputably a major breakthrough toward delineating a proper method for liturgical-sacramental study was the import of historical studies on the then recently discovered liturgical sources that preceded Trent and of the evolution of the Western liturgy itself.[4]

a. Historical Scholarship

There was and is an undisputed value to this kind of historical scholarship.[5] It broke the Tridentine deadlock on ritual inflexibility and liturgical rubricism. Most significantly, most of the post–Vatican II rites were reformed in light of such scholarship. That there was a decided preference for using the liturgy of the patristic era in structuring the present reformed liturgy is clear. What has been less clear in some catechesis "explaining" the changed rites is why.[6] I argue that some patristic "models" imaged an integration in church life, namely, that bishops preached and taught the faith as well as exercised both liturgical and pastoral leadership. An integration and harmony to church faith, life, and liturgy was presumed. Thus making the liturgies used in this period prime sources for the reform of the liturgy was an obvious and sound choice. But is there not a danger in presuming this kind of church leadership and experience, on the one hand, and of anachronism, on the other?

That there was no wish to impose a "rigid uniformity" in the revision of the liturgy is clearly enunciated in the *Constitution on the Sacred Liturgy* (no. 37). With regard to adult initiation, for example, patristic models were used but not imitated slavishly. The period of pre-revision "experimentation" with the patristic models for the catechumenate and adult initiation resulted in the present rite, noted both for its ritual richness and its flexibility. Hence, in the process of revising these rites the adage "older is better" was not necessarily operative. What was operative was mining the church's liturgical tradition for a kind of catechesis and ritual structure that was a more adequate reflection of the ecclesiology of sacramental initiation derived from historical studies (among other factors).

At the same time there are two cautions that must be noted about delineating and interpreting historical data about the evolution of Christian liturgy. The first caution concerns the fact that such data does not always reflect a linear evolution to the present (or even to Trent). That there has been diversity in the evolution of Western liturgy is clear.[7]

Among the insights that can be gleaned from studying the evolution of the Western liturgy is that there is no "golden age" of the liturgy and that when sources that preceded the Tridentine liturgy were used in the reform they were edited to suit the contemporary church's liturgical needs. What would be helpful would be some additional elaboration on why some choices were made in the reform of the liturgy (for example, a "split epiclesis" in all the post-conciliar eucharistic prayers) and to assess whether they reflect the best of all possible choices for revised rites. Such an elaboration would help to avoid the allegation of liturgical anachronism. Part of a helpful explanation would also involve how and why some Eastern liturgical sources were used in the revision of the Western liturgy.[8] To stay with the example of the epiclesis, it is certainly a major revolution in the Roman eucharistic prayers to find an explicit pneumatological epiclesis in almost all the blessing prayers revised after Vatican II, including the eucharistic prayers. That the epiclesis itself is now determined to be an intrinsic part of the eucharistic prayer structure is a major change in Western eucharistic praying (and theology).[9] To explore this rich theme theologically can help to critique some critics of the present reform of the Roman rite whose arguments are so strict in terms of liturgical history (or at least in the way they use history) that almost anything that is done today that is determined not to have been part of the evolution of the "Roman" rite is of dubious merit. This is true about texts, ritual performance, and the contents of the Tridentine rite (among other things).[10]

A second comment about history (that will lead us to the next sec-tion) concerns the general question of how we interpret liturgical his-tory. By this I mean to state that the unearthing of data about liturgical history is not sufficient. Among the questions it raises are how we inter-pret that data and what application it has for the contemporary liturgy, both in terms of present liturgical structures and the weight such histori-cal precedent has on the future shape of the liturgy, especially as the liturgy continues to be inculturated. It seems to me that the search for the "genius of the Roman rite" (to use the famous phrase of Edmund Bishop) is made more complex by the evidence of liturgical history, namely, that what some may call the Roman rite did in fact come from other Western sources and practices (the merging of Gallican and Roman practices is a most clear example), and that some elements of the liturgy, specifically music and architecture, are evidence of how inculturation was part and parcel of the Western liturgy's evolution. What weight, then, does one give to a particular style of architecture or music or liturgical practice when it derives from various periods in the evolution of the liturgy? My suspicion is that in the reform of the liturgy some practices from the tradition were judged more valuable in sustaining a kind of vision about and of the liturgy that Vatican II enunciated. But questions remain as to the relative weight to be placed on periods, authors, and practices in the evolution of liturgical history and why. In addition, some of the extremes in contemporary liturgical literature today would either mitigate the notion of a "Roman rite" or argue that the present reforms and experience of the liturgy are far from their Roman roots (which often means Tridentine) and that the present reform is misguided.[11]

b. Liturgical Theology

Thanks to the revival of the adage *lex orandi, lex credendi,* both before and after Vatican II, the liturgy's theological depth and value have regained prominence in liturgical study. In fact, one could argue that in large measure the present discussions about the adequacy of vernacular translations of the liturgy concern the application and interpretation of this principle. Since what we pray is what we believe, then what we pray ought to be as theologically precise as possible, understanding that liturgical texts are of their nature poetic and filled with images and metaphors. Nonetheless, they need to be theologically precise. My own suspicion is that the present rhetoric about the translation of liturgical texts emphasizing inculturation and inclusivity deserves a more substantial base that would make discussions about them less politicizing. This could well be supplied by emphasizing the theological import of what we say and do liturgically. The debates should really be about the formative value of what we pray liturgically. When the issue of adequacy in liturgical texts (for example, the second edition of the Roman Missal) focuses on accuracy of translation for the sake of an adequate representation of the faith of the church, then debates about vernacular translations are better grounded and (it is to be hoped) more disciplined.

That part of the revived interest in liturgical theology derives from European authors and sources is clear. Recall such names as I. H.

Dalmais, Louis Bouyer, Cipriano Vagaggini, Salvatore Marsili, Gerard Lukken, and Albert Houssiau.[12] That it has been carried out admirably by contemporary American authors across the ecumenical spectrum is reflected in the work of people like Alexander Schmemann, Geoffrey Wainwright, Aidan Kavanagh, Peter Fink, Edward Kilmartin, David Power, Mary Collins, and Gordon Lathrop.[13] That the scope of an adequate method for liturgical theology is broad and that in the post-conciliar era we have probably many more questions than answers about what constitutes liturgical theology attest to the importance of this question today and to the possible range of issues involved.[14] That significant inroads have been made in the contemporary magisterium by the theology derived from the liturgy is seen in the way the *Catechism of the Catholic Church* articulates its theology of sacraments. The section "Baptism in the Economy of Salvation" is structured on the prayer used to bless water during the rite (nos. 1217–22). Other blessing prayers for individual sacraments are frequently cited (for example, confirmation, no. 1299), and the theology of the structure and content of the eucharistic prayer (nos. 1352–55) underscores the assertion in the *General Instruction of the Roman Missal* that the high point in the eucharistic celebration is the proclamation of the eucharistic prayer (no. 78).[15] That such initiatives deserve greater elaboration in theologies of and about sacraments is clear. That such initiatives are reflected in magisterial literature, albeit somewhat sparingly, is to be welcomed.[16]

One immediate application of this emphasis on liturgical theology can enhance sacramental catechesis when what is taught both reflects and is reflected in what is celebrated liturgically. Here the issue of integration comes to the fore: Integrating what we do catechetically with what we enact liturgically can go a long way toward bridging a perceived "disconnect" between these, and chief "sources" for this are the revised liturgical rites from Vatican II. (In engaging in this task the frameworks provided by the authors just cited can be enormously helpful.)

What makes this task the more challenging in the face of the present revised liturgy is the fact that the present rites envision and enjoy a flexibility within liturgical structures. This is to say, the fixed rites of the former Tridentine liturgy could yield rather fixed results theologically precisely because the rites were fixed. Given the flexibility of the revised rites, however, one needs to take into consideration that what one experiences liturgically may in fact stretch or alter the meanings inherent in the revised liturgy. What happens when what occurs in the liturgy (I use the term *lex agendi* to describe this) is at variance with what the revised rites envision? Or what happens when some of the gestures or music of a given liturgy are not in harmony with the theological vision presumed in the revised rites? Precisely because liturgical rites are enacted they affect those who celebrate them. *Lex orandi* thus concerns much more than texts in a revised rite. It concerns a number of things in which people engage in the act of liturgy. And these have an impact on our consciousness of what the rites mean theologically. It would seem that at the very least a consideration of criteria for what occurs in any act of liturgy should derive from the revised rites.

Yet at the same time that we are engaged in the legitimate (not to say urgent) task of unpacking the present reformed liturgy theologically, there are voices that appropriately critique the present revisions on a number of bases. That the task of liturgical theology today involves a critique of the present rites is fairly commonly appreciated.[17] In fact, one could say that this is what distinguishes liturgical theology from liturgical catechesis. Catechesis takes what is and explores its theology. Liturgical theology explores both a catechesis about what exists in the liturgy and ways that the revised liturgy might be better adapted and inculturated to suit contemporary congregations.

At present there are a number of theological issues that in my opinion have been underdeveloped theologically; they derive from the theological foundations of the revision of the present liturgy. Two examples concern active participation in the liturgy. Clearly "full, conscious, active participation" was a clarion call in the revision of the liturgy after Vatican II. Legitimately, the engagement of all those who participate in the liturgy has been emphasized in the implementation of the post-conciliar liturgical rites. My concern is whether this exemplification of what *participation* means is balanced by adequate theological exposition of what it means to participate in the sense of "to take part in" the very life of the triune God in the liturgical action within the church as community. The challenge here is to emphasize both the externals of participation and the meaning of what that external activity means in terms of appropriating the paschal mystery in the body of Christ.

In addition, it seems to me that work is needed on the theological meaning of what the magisterium and the liturgy repeatedly assert regarding the role of the celebrating church in the act of offering the eucharistic sacrifice. Some contemporary assertions about the a priori separations between what the priest offers and what the church offers in the liturgy need to be informed by what the *Constitution on the Sacred Liturgy* states:

> The Church, therefore, earnestly desires that Christ's faithful, when present at this mystery of faith, should not be there as strangers or silent spectators. On the contrary, through a proper appreciation of the rites and prayers they should participate knowingly, devoutly, and actively. They should be instructed by God's word and be refreshed at the table of the Lord's body; they should give thanks to God; by offering the Immaculate Victim, not only through the hands of the priest, but also with him, they should learn to offer themselves too. Through Christ the mediator, they should be drawn day by day into ever closer union with God and with each other, so that finally God may be all in all (no. 48).

c. Aesthetics

At the beginning of this section I indicated that the twentieth century could be regarded as *the* century of liturgical-sacramental method. As it ended, the century left us with enormously important vistas for inclusion into what liturgical method is about. At the risk of oversimplification I suggest that an overarching theme for much of what has emerged as constitutive of liturgical method and of what still needs further refinement as constitutive of liturgical method concerns a "liturgical aesthetic." Simply put, liturgy is art, and the arts are constitutive of every act of liturgy. Put positively, this means that aesthetics needs to be factored into the method of liturgical study precisely because it constitutes one essential element of what the liturgy is and does. Put somewhat negatively, I suspect that many of the contemporary arguments over music, architecture, and the arts used in worship deserve greater depth and a clearer articulation of their rightful place in the liturgy. As part of the process of implementing the revised liturgy the U.S. Bishops' Committee on the Liturgy took proper and important leadership in issuing documents to guide the implementation on the liturgy regarding music (*Music in Catholic Worship* in 1972, *Liturgical Music Today* in 1982, and *Environment and Art in Catholic Worship* in 1978). That aspects of these documents have been found wanting today should not be regarded as an invitation to jettison or to ignore them. They deserve attention and, where needed, nuancing and improvement.

Symptomatic of greater concern for the place of the arts in liturgy today is the debate in liturgical music circles between proponents of the statement from the Milwaukee symposia on liturgy and music and the authors and proponents of the "Snowbird Statement."[18] Admittedly, some of what is debated here concerns the intention and theology of the reformed liturgy, for example, the place of hymns in the Roman eucharistic liturgy (an issue about which I myself am admittedly less than impartial).[19] But some of the debate has to do with the notion of aesthetics and the role of the arts in crafting, celebrating, and experiencing the reformed liturgy. In addition, there are obvious issues about the notion of proper church architecture, specifically in the United States about the enduring value of the document *Environment and Art in Catholic Worship,* especially as it is placed alongside similar texts from other episcopal conferences (such as *The Parish Church* from the Irish Episcopal Conference and *The Building and Reorganisation of Church Buildings* from the Episcopal Conference of England and Wales). The recent debates about the document to supplement *Environment and Art in Catholic Worship, Made of Living Stones* (formally called *Domus Dei*) indicate high interest in the formative value of church art and architecture. It is to be hoped that these debates and the document will reflect that a church building is both a "house for the church" and a building whose beauty and construction reflect both the transcendence and the immanence of the God worshiped within it.[20]

My concern is that legitimate debates about style and taste not becloud some of the theological bases on which the use of arts in worship is based; namely, that the arts reflect the genius of human creativity offered to God in service of the church. The theological principle is that human creativity, productivity, and labor are offered to God when the arts are used in worship. The arts have to do with the genius of the human spirit, creativity, and nonverbal ways of relating to and engaging in the worship of God.[21]

2. LITURGICAL REFORM AND RENEWAL: IMPLEMENTED AND UNFINISHED

The purpose of this section is to invite reflection on positive aspects of the present liturgical reform and on areas in which the implementation of the reform needs attention both in theory and practice. Here I would like to distinguish *liturgical reform* from *liturgical renewal.* Liturgical reform can be accomplished by changing the externals of the liturgy from those of the Tridentine liturgy to those of the present reformed liturgy. For the most part I think it accurate to say that most of the intended reforms of the liturgy after Vatican II have been implemented and are in place. One can only marvel at the amount of time, energy, and creativity that has been expended since Vatican II on accomplishing the tasks involved in reforming the liturgy.

Major structural adjustments in our churches to suit the revised liturgy in general (place and shape of ambo, altar, font and chair, for example) were matched by major changes in the books and artifacts used for the celebration of the reformed liturgy and in training a plethora of ministers to lead parts or all of the reformed rites from these revised rites. The very expansion of liturgical roles attests to a new ecclesiological vision to be reflected in all liturgical rites, which are always communal celebrations with a variety of ministers involved (*Constitution on the Sacred Liturgy,* nos. 27–28).

These liturgical reforms had to be accompanied by catechesis and formation because by its nature the present reform of the liturgy has structural elements that change and the rites themselves have a certain flexibility built into them (choices for readings from the lectionaries, choices for prayer texts, newly composed prayers such as the prayer of the faithful, amount and kind of music, and so on). To exercise liturgical ministry with an invariable rite has its own challenges; to exercise such ministry with rites that are flexible requires much greater skill and familiarity with the rites. When one focuses on liturgical renewal, however, one then needs to focus on what these reforms are meant to "accomplish" (taken from the phrase *opus nostrae redemptionis exercetur,* meaning that in the liturgy "the word of our redemption is accomplished"). Part of this concerns the way the liturgical reforms are carried out, for which one needs to be attentive to, among other things, the manifold presence of Christ in the liturgy, how the church encounters Christ in the liturgy, and the kind of conversion one needs to bring to the liturgy and the way that initial conversion is deepened (or not) through the liturgy. Hence, it is one thing to proclaim readings from a revised lectionary with a large range of scripture readings, responsorial psalms, and so on, and quite another to appropriate what those texts say and mean. This is where the reform of the liturgy is meant to serve ongoing conversion and church renewal. On one level this concerns what *happens* when the scriptures are proclaimed at the liturgy and the *effect* that proclamation has on those who hear them. In a parallel way one can assert that the reform of the eucharistic rite concerns changes in sacramentary texts and gestures as engaged in by the whole assembly as well as priest, deacon, acolyte, eucharistic ministers, and so on. Once again, it is one thing to change texts and rites and quite another to determine whether those changes are reflected in attitudes about eucharistic *presence,* eucharistic *action,* and eucharistic theology. If, in fact, the eucharistic prayer is the high point of the entire eucharistic celebration,[22] the issue for eucharistic theology is whether and how what is proclaimed about the Eucharist as a dynamic, involving action is reflected in eucharistic theology, one aspect of which concerns the extent to which what is said is reflected in how believers reflect this kind of theology in their lives.

a. Where Are We Today?

At present, initiatives continue both here and from Rome concerning the ongoing reform of the liturgy. That a new Latin and English study translation edition of the *General Instruction of the Roman Missal* has been published, a new edition of the *Sacramentary for Mass* is awaited, feasts have been added to the calendar, and there is likelihood of a fifth (Latin) volume of the *Liturgia Horarum* all reflect the existence of ongoing liturgical reforms. Not all such initiatives, however, are met with overwhelming support (for example, whether the second Sunday of Easter should be termed Divine Mercy Sunday is cause for no small consternation in liturgical circles today).

Concerns are raised today about what one might call the tone or style of the celebration of the present reformed liturgy. Some liturgical revisions shocked people—for example, Mass with the priest facing the people, wearing white instead of black vestments at funerals, and the use of reconciliation rooms instead of the confessional box for the sacrament of penance. In addition, at present there are voices urging a "reform of the reform" or a mitigation of the reform. For example, last February Bishop David Foley of Birmingham, Alabama, requested clarification from the Congregation of Divine Worship about whether there is a preference about celebrating the Mass *ad orientem* or *versus populum,* and whether the eucharistic prayers added to the Roman euchology after Vatican II carry the same weight as the "traditional" Roman canon. The prefect's response was not surprising. He cited the relevant texts of the *General Instruction of the Roman Missal* and stated that these citations "foresee that the priest will face the body of people in the nave while leaving open the possibility of his celebrating toward the apse."[23] With regard to the eucharistic prayers introduced into the Roman rite by Pope Paul VI, the prefect indicated that the three additional prayers were to be considered lawful and that liturgical law gives no gradation with respect to orthodoxy. "There is therefore no question of the first eucharistic prayer or Roman Canon being 'more orthodox' than the others and such an idea is without any foundation." Even these recent remarks of the prefect, however, seem not to have ended the debate; Cardinal Ratzinger has raised the issue of Mass *ad orientem* in a recent publication.[24]

Without wishing to draw undue attention to this issue of the location of the altar, it is still worth probing what is meant when the location of the priest changes dramatically from back to the people to facing the people. While the recent rhetoric speaks about *ad orientem,* it is curious that almost immediately the emphasis shifts in some writing to notions of "transcendence" and the priest not facing the people becomes the issue. Classically, the issue was the pilgrim church facing east awaiting Christ's second coming. Now, at least for some, the reason the priest's back is to the congregation is to emphasize anonymity and transcendence. According to the *General Instruction of the Roman Missal* the altar is to be "freestanding to allow the ministers to walk around it easily and Mass to be celebrated facing the people which is desirable whenever possible" (no. 299). Obviously, this assertion as well as the prescriptions about the location of the ambo, font and presider's chair all make theological statements. They are part of the church's *lex orandi,* and therefore are part of our *lex credendi.*

At the same time, there are some hopes and disappointments

about liturgical reform that need to be named and addressed. Issues about a sense of reverence and the transcendent ought not to be dismissed out of hand as old fashioned or mean spirited. The fact that the present reformed liturgy requires careful planning and celebration (as reiterated by John Paul II in *Dies Domini*, no. 50) does raise the question about an adequate tone and style for the celebration of the liturgy. "One size" does not fit all liturgical circumstances. Nor do assertions about beauty and transcendence. The liturgy is also a time and place; it values ecclesial relatedness to Christ and to one another. A delicate balance should be struck between the transcendent and the immanent, between otherness and the here and now of our redemption. My own sense is that some of the more contentious debates that occur at present could well be termed today's liturgy wars, with hardened positions and factions lined up according to preconceived ideologies. More often than not these "wars" rage about the externals of the *reform* of the liturgy. What would be highly desirable today would be the establishment of a forum in which issues about the present malaise in both the liturgical *reform* and liturgical *renewal* could be addressed.

For example, given the comparative success of the implementation of the Order for Christian Funerals, might it not be opportune to raise the question about the adequacy of having changed from black to white vesture when in fact the rite admits that other liturgical colors (such as violet) might better reflect the paschal and passage nature of these rites? Or, given the architecture of some church buildings, could there ever be a situation in which the altar in a given church should remain "against the wall" for the simple reason that it was designed that way centuries ago for the Tridentine liturgy or because placing an additional altar in the center of the sanctuary might mitigate the kind of movement required in the celebration of the reformed liturgy? The kind of irenic tone that such legitimate debates deserve is not always reflected in the literature today, with passions running high on all sides.

In a sense we ought not be surprised that liturgy evokes such emotions. I argue, however, that today's liturgy wars really are surface issues and that what lies behind some of them are questions about the value of Vatican II itself as a reform council, the scope of local church authority vis-à-vis Rome, and the nature and scope of Catholicism itself as a theological tradition (as opposed to a fundamentalist group that merely repeats older formulas and uses old forms of prayer). Unfortunately, not to challenge the contemporary liturgy wars would be tantamount to giving in to the shape and scope of the former Tridentine liturgy and Tridentine liturgical theology. This is to ask whether the present preoccupation with the externals of liturgy really reflects the kind of liturgical and church reform the council intended by revising the liturgy. That the *Constitution on the Sacred Liturgy* began by asserting that "the goal of this most sacred Council [is] to intensify the daily growth of Catholics in Christian living [and] to make more responsive to the requirements of our times those Church observances which are open to adaptation" (no. 1) should cause us pause when so much effort today concerns liturgy's externals. In effect, cannot one ask whether many contemporary debates about liturgy reflect a reform at all and whether the terms of the debate are exactly the same as those of the Tridentine liturgy? Might one ask whether much of the current superficial warfare avoids the real issue of liturgical renewal? In other words, what is easier, to change rites or to renew lives?

b. Unfinished Liturgical Reforms

In one sense, given the scope of the liturgical changes that have been undertaken since Vatican II, we will likely continue to see revisions and consolidations of rites already in existence (for example, rites for adult initiation incorporated into the liturgy for the Easter Vigil in the revised *Sacramentary for Mass*). At the same time some of the presently existing rites require attention and implementation, for example, the daily celebration of the Liturgy of the Hours. Many argue that the present reform of the Hours is too unwieldy for parish use and that simpler forms in publications designed for the plethora of church communities need to be developed. I think this is largely true. One key unresolved issue, however, concerns an inclusive-language psalter. The fact that the ICEL Psalter project is not approved for official liturgical use means that another approach needs to be taken so that the psalter can be used pastorally. In effect, a decision about the psalter would also affect the texts of the responsorial psalms for all the liturgical lectionaries as well as the entrance and communion antiphons at Mass. One disappointment with the present liturgical reform as envisioned by the council and in the revised rites is precisely the absence of regular daily celebration of the

Hours. This is a great lack, especially given the interest in prayer forms and spirituality today. This biblically based traditional prayer form can be celebrated without the leadership of the ordained. Popular versions could become a staple of prayer in the home, classroom, and elsewhere.

I am not sure that the overwhelmingly positive reaction to communal celebrations of the anointing of the sick was envisioned when the *Rite of Anointing and Pastoral Care of the Sick* was first published. But in fact where communal anointings are celebrated regularly they have received almost universal acclaim as sources of comfort, hope, and strength—all elements that taken together constitute true healing. Unfortunately, the same cannot be said for the three forms of sacramental penance and the one form of a non-sacramental liturgy of penance in the revised rite of penance. At a time when people have claimed the anointing of the sick as a rite of healing, one can only wonder what the future is of communal celebrations of penance. It seems that when the rite of penance was first published there was a conflict about where and when the third form of sacramental penance with general absolution would take place. The progressive limitation of the frequency with which this rite can be used has caused the first two rites to be the only ones commonly celebrated. Often this means individual confessions and occasional (Advent and Lent?) communal celebrations with individual absolution. Does this state of practice really reflect the theology of the *General Instruction on the Rite of Penance*? Does it really reflect the theology and import of the proclamation of the word of God as constitutive of the act of sacramental reconciliation? And, at the risk of seeming to take the priests' side in this forum, I often wonder whether the way priests travel from parish to parish in the two or three weeks before Christmas and Easter for nightly celebrations of the second rite was really envisioned as the way to prepare for these feasts.

One instance of consolidating rites and perhaps looking for further refinement concerns the Easter triduum itself. My suspicion is that the triduum as we have it stands in line with the reforms of Holy Week undertaken by Pius XII in 1951 and 1956. But they are not without problems. One concerns distinguishing "dramatization" from liturgical engagement, exemplified in the washing of the feet at the Evening Mass of the Lord's Supper. While most of the publicity surrounding foot washing over the past fifteen years in this country has concerned whether women's feet can be washed (given the rubric *viri selecti*), the 1987 statement of the Bishops' Committee on the Liturgy asserting that this is possible is still in force. From a theological perspective much of the controversy about washing feet may well have drawn attention away from other more central elements of this liturgy: sharing gifts with the poor and emphasizing the Eucharist itself as the central mystery of this night with appropriate eucharistic devotion to follow the liturgy and this evening liturgy itself as the overture to the triduum as the church's annual immersion into the totality of Christ's dying and rising (not "just" the institution of the Eucharist). It is in this context that issues about the theology of the ordained priesthood and the washing of the feet should be placed. My point is that the Roman rite was slow to adopt the rite of foot washing; that is, it has always been optional and has never officially adopted liturgical texts at this liturgy that refer to ministerial priesthood. I argue that the reason is that liturgy is always a multivalent celebration and that to draw attention to only one or another aspect would be to collapse the interdependence of several themes that are celebrated at liturgy at the same time. This danger can be called "dramatization" of one aspect of the liturgy over against engagement in the range of symbols inherent in all liturgy. Specifically, this means that any overemphasis on whose feet can be washed detracts from other central aspects of the liturgy such as the theology of linking Eucharist with service for the poor, which is far more traditional than is the relatively recent (and optional) custom of washing feet.[25]

While not the subject of this same kind of emotional tug of war, there is the question of the present breadth of the Easter Vigil. My interpretation of liturgical history is that the Roman rite has never before had an Easter Vigil with the number of elements and the breadth of ritual we have today. The specific pastoral issue is how to do justice to the service of light, word, initiation, and Eucharist all at the same time. Given the success of programs for the formation of catechumens and candidates, it is fairly common to experience celebrations of the vigil that are so focused on initiation that they eclipse other aspects of the liturgy for this night. These include the way the liturgy articulates a theology of creation of the world by God and its annual recreation through the rites of fire and word at the vigil and the fact that initiation leads to the celebration of the Eucharist as the term of the process of preparation and initiation itself. Part of my concern is that no one element of a given liturgy dominate and that dramatization not eclipse sacramental celebration.

In general, an important question for the pastoral implementation of the liturgy is how much one liturgy can be expected to do. Something of the conventional expectation of the Roman rite is that its being comparatively spare fosters emphasis on what is essential and distinguishes this from what is peripheral. Especially in parishes liturgy planners find themselves negotiating a number of values when planning and celebrating the Sunday liturgy: children's liturgy of the word, catechumenal dismissals, dismissal of eucharistic ministers, stewardship (and other second collections) talks, the need for liturgical catechesis, and more. Given all these quite legitimate concerns related to the Sunday liturgy, how much can one liturgy do?

c. Agenda for Liturgical Renewal

To paraphrase Aidan Kavanagh, the liturgy is too important to be left to the liturgists. Liturgy is a chief characteristic of Catholicism. If it is, in fact, the "summit and source" of the church's life, then energies need to be expended on relating liturgy to life, specifically to the renewal of the very life of the church in all its variations and contexts. The keys to any agenda for true liturgical renewal, it seems to me, are a theologically informed spirituality and catechesis.

For example, the reform of liturgical ministries should be precisely about *ministry* for and in the context of the church. They should not simply be about *ministers*—who they are and their legitimate liturgical roles. Once the wider context of church life is the focus, then what matters is how liturgical ministers serve the church both in liturgical celebration and in the entire life of faith of the church community. Emphasis is then placed on eucharistic ministers serving the Eucharist at the liturgy and taking communion to the homebound. Readers proclaim the word in liturgy and are evangelizers and catechists. Deacons serve at the altar as well as in the many and varied ways that the church's charity dictates outside the liturgy. If and when this kind of emphasis on the broad contours of church life and ministry occurs, a "spirituality" for ministers is taken care of; preoccupation with liturgy as rite cedes to focusing on liturgy as a means to express our faith in life and as a lens through which we evaluate and experience our life of faith.

With regard to catechesis specifically, my sense is that emphasizing the *lex orandi* can only help to ground what we believe in what we say and do liturgically. This means that more adequate translations of the reformed liturgy are crucial precisely because the vernacular liturgy is so formative. My own sense is that there will be a significant upheaval when the revised *Sacramentary for Mass* is published, precisely because familiar but inadequate phrases in the euchology will, of necessity, be dropped. (For example, the phrase in the third eucharisic prayer "from east to west a perfect offering may be made" will be rendered more literally: "from the rising of the sun to its setting a pure offering may be made to the glory of your name.") This is a negative way of saying that what we pray has an impact on believers' faith lives and imaginations. To change them will require catechesis.

Far more urgent is the need for a sacramental catechesis based on the revised rites—their structure, ecclesial presuppositions, and actual texts. This would help bridge any perceived "disconnect" between what we say and do catechetically and what we say and do liturgically. At the same time an overriding issue concerns what may be called a spirituality derived from the liturgy. Such a spirituality might well be decidedly counter-cultural today, in that ecclesial belonging and liturgical participation presume that we take one another seriously as brothers and sisters in the family of the faith of the church. True Christian spirituality reflected in the liturgy will always be about the good of the whole body of Christ, not just the self.

For example, a eucharistic catechesis that is truly integral and formative should emphasize that the Eucharist is an ecclesial act done by and for the whole church. Emphases on the manifold presence of Christ as experienced both in the eucharistic liturgy and in all of daily life could help to refocus an overemphasis on eucharistic elements only. The principle of analogy can be utilized here to give due emphasis both to the eucharistic presence of Christ and to the church as the body of Christ built up by the sacrament of the Lord's body and blood. Without such an integral approach I am concerned that what will result is a catechesis of new wine in old wineskins.

Another way to help overcome the "disconnect" between patterns of liturgical prayer and devotional prayers would be to recast patterns of domestic prayer and piety away from devotions that are not in accord with the liturgy to domestic prayer that emphasizes elements of the liturgy itself. Obvious examples include Bible reading, using the psalms as much as possible, intercessory prayers derived from the scriptures, and table blessings. These practices can familiarize people with the riches of the liturgy on a scale that is appropriable and that invites deeper and richer probing. But even here these means, as important as they are, should be regarded as precisely that, means toward accomplishing what only God can accomplish among us: deeper conversion of mind and heart and the building up of the church as community and as communion.

In the end the ultimate purpose of the liturgy is to help us put real life and what really matters in life into perspective. This means that the liturgy as familiar patterns of ritual behavior unleashes the power of God in ever new and often unexpected ways. One temptation for those of us engaged in the planning and celebration of the liturgy is to domesticate the liturgy and to resist its confounding power to change us into the people God calls us to be. Emphasizing liturgy's externals can belie our individual and collective fear that the liturgy is ultimately subversive and dangerous because its intended effect might well require that we change, and change often. In this perspective liturgy is not an escape from this life and world but a vision that helps us penetrate and experience God both here and now and in the kingdom. It is prophetic in that it always challenges us to deeper conversion, and it is also proleptic in that it always requires that we look beyond the here and now to liturgy's fulfillment in the kingdom of heaven.

3. LITURGICAL AND SACRAMENTAL RHETORIC AND REALITY

a. Sacramental Preparation

Though the Public Broadcasting Service series on Vatican II asserted again and again that it was the changes in the liturgy of the Mass that put a face on the reforms of Vatican II, I believe that it has been the pastoral implementation of the *Rite of Christian Initiation of Adults (RCIA)* that has put a face on the way parishes prepare for and celebrate the sacraments, not only of adult initiation but also of most other "first" sacraments. Sacramental preparation programs began springing up at the time of the council, but it has been the implementation of the *RCIA* that has given these programs shape, focus, and stability as staples of parish life. The process enshrined in adult initiation has become something of a pastoral norm and therefore has been the most obvious and far-reaching sacramental change in terms of the pastoral practice since Vatican II.

In a real sense there is no such thing as simply a liturgical change; liturgical changes necessarily affect other areas of theology and church life. This is certainly true for the rites of adult initiation. The periods of inquiry and the catechumenate emphasize discernment, prayer, catechesis, and apostolic work, all undertaken with a range of mentors and ministers, sponsors and sponsoring parishes. The rite of election and the scrutinies mark the Lenten liturgical calendar of most parishes. The Easter Vigil takes on newfound meaning from the reintroduction of adult initiation as a high point. A number of questions need to be asked, however, about both the RCIA process and about sacramental preparation in parishes in general. To introduce this topic I want to turn to what is often less emphasized in liturgical-sacramental circles but remains at the heart of pastoral sacramental ministry today—marriage.

Succinctly put, major theological and pastoral questions surround how to minister to baptized nonbelievers or the baptized who do not practice their faith. Despite these obvious factors in church life today, we teach and practice that the baptized have a "right" to Christian marriage. Significant pastoral attention was given to this precise set of questions in the mid 1970s in France with abundant literature available on pastoral strategies and canonical accommodations (specifically some Catholics did not celebrate a sacramental marriage but were "welcomed" to the household of the faith).[26]

Among the liturgical issues surrounding marriage is the question of whether a nuptial Eucharist should be the norm for the celebration of Christian marriage. With the decline in the number of priests in some areas, the wedding Eucharist is sometimes celebrated at a Sunday Mass. Or sometimes couples forego a Eucharist because of issues of intercommunion. Or again, there is the frustration felt by parish ministers when couples who request a wedding Eucharist have minimal catechesis about what the Eucharist is and the assembly needs to be prompted to participate.

Canonically, there are significant issues surrounding former marriages, annulments, dispensations, and so on. Pastorally, there are issues about couples cohabitating before marriage and the amount of money couples choose to spend on lavish parties, receptions, and other trappings. One can only wonder whether our rhetoric about sacraments is really disconnected from the reality of the sacramental celebration of marriage today. According to liturgical tradition, evangelization leads to initiation which leads to a sacramental marriage. Today it is not uncommon for parish staffs to engage baptized couples in evangelization when they come to prepare for their weddings. How common is it that one of the key pastoral opportunities for what John Paul II calls "the new evangelization" takes place at just such moments of sacramental preparation? In the face of such pastoral challenges, parishes and dioceses engage in significant preparation programs for marriage. But how much of this is "too little, too late," especially when couples come to these programs with attitudes already formed about what they expect from the church. And some would question today how much the church can or should require of couples presenting themselves for marriage or for any other sacrament.

When it comes to preparation for other sacraments, issues abound about how many "sessions" should be required and in what these should consist. Adrien Nocent makes a very good case for incorporating ritual and prayer elements into the preparation for infant baptism. Basing himself on the way the adult scrutinies were condensed into the *Gelasian Sacramentary* for infants before water baptism, Nocent offers a creative approach to baptismal preparation incorporating catechesis for the parents and exorcisms for the children, all done in a communal setting.[27] That all too often such preparations sessions for infant baptism are perceived to be obligatory diminishes some of the potential such opportunities offer for enlivening the faith of parents.

b. Sacramental Hostage-Taking?

One of the more difficult challenges in sacramental circles today concerns what to do with post-baptismal confirmation. Debates about the age for confirmation recur in the U.S. Bishops' Conference with some regularity. The "resolution," at least to this point, is to agree to disagree. Some dioceses have recently placed confirmation along with first Eucharist as a unified celebration (Portland, Maine; Yakima, Washington; and others). This has its pros and cons. At the very same time, however, some dioceses that changed confirmation to a late high school rite of passage have found this practice to be pastorally beneficial. Simply put, students have to comply with a one- or two-year preparation program that offers them evangelization and catechesis at an important time of their life. In effect, one can make a case for the pastoral usefulness of preparation for confirmation at whatever age, admitting varying degrees of benefit.

Yet one needs to raise the question of whether some sacramental preparation programs, especially for confirmation, are perceived to be "tasks" one must perform in order to celebrate that sacrament. In other words, are sacramental preparation programs a new Pelagianism? Canonically, it is certainly true that the bar for sacraments is quite low. One can only wonder whether one of the issues about confirmation concerns its theology and whether the lack of a theology of confirmation separate from water baptism is not the cause of preparation programs that obfuscate the specific theology of confirmation and emphasize themes common to the whole of the Christian life. But again, the question of whether we hold candidates for sacraments "hostage" is worth reflection, as is the question of whether sacramental preparation is the current way to "earn" sacraments.

c. Liturgical Time-keeping

It seems clear that the liturgical calendar and the notion of a liturgical year are both out for repairs. A major source of the conflict concerns principles undergirding the liturgical calendar over against contemporary liturgical practices. At the same time, one can state quite rightly that our culture's use of Monday holidays has done its own damage to anniversaries and precise memorials.

The advent of Saturday evening Masses has been a pastoral boon for many people, and it is almost universally practiced. But can the down-side be that Sunday as a qualitatively different day of the week is eclipsed and regarded as just another day of commerce or filled with the normal range of daily activities? The theology of Sunday as *the* primary liturgical feast day commemorating our incorporation into Christ's paschal mystery through the Eucharist has itself suffered because of placing such celebrations as the Epiphany and Corpus Christi on Sundays, and now in many parts of the United States Ascension is celebrated on a Sunday.

The whole question of days of precept (days of obligation) deserves revisiting. The present assignment of days as obligatory except when they fall on a Monday or Saturday has failed. Similarly, the frequency and popularity of Masses celebrated on Christmas Eve diminishes the theology of Christmas itself, primarily because the Vigil Mass was never intended to take the place of the traditional celebration of Christmas day with its traditional texts of Hebrews 1 and the prologue of John's gospel.

On a positive note, I do think that the intention of restoring initiation and reconciliation themes to Lent has been successful, and that Lent as a time of initial conversion for catechumens and of deepened conversion for the already initiated is supported both in church rhetoric and liturgical reality. But challenges do abound with regard to the calendar, for example, the relative weight given to female and male saints commemorated as well as the relative balance between religious and clergy, on the one hand, and laypersons on the other.

4. CONFIDENCE IN THE LITURGY

Up until now I have expressed some of the hopes and disappointments from within the Catholic Church about the reform and the renewal of the liturgy. There are, however, forces outside the church today (and, I would hasten to add, all the mainline liturgical churches) that challenge the presumption of the value of liturgy itself. The clearest example is the phenomenon of the mega-churches. Sunday worship services in them are dramatic representations of scenes from daily life that often end with a moral or inspirational twist highlighting a value one should incorporate into one's life. Liturgical principles and ritual structures thus cede to "relevance" and the "quick fix." Don Saliers has recently quipped that we ought to call this what it is—para-liturgical entertainment. And yet there are at least three issues that relate to the success of this phenomenon that are worth reflection: dramatization, liturgical structures, and God's initiative in all liturgy.

a. Dramatization

I offered above some observations about the dramatization of the washing of the feet taking precedence over other more legitimate themes of the Evening Mass of the Lord's Supper. I should like to elaborate on this a bit further here by raising the question about the role of this kind of tableau when it comes to passion plays on Good Friday or a children's pageant at vigil Masses for Christmas. These practices exemplify the same issue as foot-washing on Holy Thursday, namely, that liturgy's inherent multivalence can be eclipsed (almost always with very good intentions) and that one theme can dominate over the many that the liturgy always celebrates. This is to suggest that one of the real problems with a children's pageant acting out the details of the gospel of the Christmas Vigil is that such dramatizations can force one to recall the past and freeze one's imagination on Jesus' birth at Bethlehem when all liturgy is inherently about the paschal mystery and all liturgy always has an eschatological thrust. Simply put, we need to be very cautious about what we plan and project onto a liturgy that might mitigate its true theological roots.

The same thing is true for passion plays on Good Friday or the stations of the cross. These are specific dramatizations of aspects of how Jesus died for our salvation. But again, these are not part of the church's liturgy of Good Friday for the theological reason that dramatizing one aspect of the mystery over others can skew what is offered and perceived to be occurring at liturgy itself. In the end we are a liturgical and sacramental church. The way we appropriate and experience the paschal mystery is through liturgy's regularly repeated rhythms and patterns—through sacramental liturgy, not drama. Having confidence in the liturgy's ritual structures is crucial. Even when we argue for adjustments in the liturgy, we always need to recall that it is the liturgy itself we are critiquing, not some drama or devotion that some might want to see "connected" to it.

b. Liturgical Structures

That there is a rhyme and reason, an inherent logic, to the liturgy should be obvious and should be clear in celebration. That we sometimes want to "make up for what is lacking" in these structures can mitigate confidence in them and in what God accomplishes through them. From the perspective of the religious educator especially, there can be a kind of passionate pastoral zeal that wants to ensure the liturgy's impact and value. This is all to the good, provided that the liturgy's ritual structure is respected.

In this connection the works of Marva Dawn are fascinating, challenging, and useful.[28] She continually emphasizes the pedagogical value of the liturgy and emphasizes liturgy's theological depth and meaning. Rather than reinvent the liturgy, Dawn regularly points out that catechesis about the liturgy and domestic patterns of prayer that reflect the liturgy can emphasize how liturgy is the true jewel in the crown of the mainline churches. The inherent logic of the proclamation of the word, leading to intercessions and then to sacramental enactment, provides the background for most of what Dawn argues. (Her implicit critiques of the mega-church phenomenon are irenic and encouraging.)

One of the real challenges for the liturgical churches, however, is how to provide worship services that are both respectful of the liturgical tradition and yet are invitational and relevant to the daily life of worshipers. The challenge, it seems to me, is not to adjust ritual structures precisely because they are just that—structured rituals. The challenge is how to celebrate them in such a way that connections are made between what we do in them and what occurs in daily life. A major burden is then placed on preaching, music, and hospitality. No one can predict or plan the impact of these aspects of every liturgy. Yet in the end, these are likely among the most memorable things that the liturgy offers. These elements of liturgy cannot be programmed. They need special attention and care, all done within respect for the structures of the liturgy itself.

c. Divine Initiative

If one were to contrast the past forty years of liturgical change and evolution with the previous four hundred years, one could legitimately say that we have more recently been self-conscious about liturgy: what to say and do and how to enact it. This is all quite legitimate; in fact, it has been required by the reform of the liturgy. But I do wonder whether this aspect of liturgical engagement should have run its course by now and whether we ought not to focus on the kind of deeper liturgical renewal in spirituality, catechesis, and theology that this chapter has tried to underscore. The techniques and performance aspects of liturgy are important as the frame within which the divine action inherent in the liturgy happens. In the end, liturgy is primarily about what God does among us and for us. All that we do in the liturgy is but a response to the overarching, grace-filled initiative of God. I sometimes also wonder whether emphasizing what "we do" in the liturgy is a particularly American phenomenon and preoccupation. The phrases of the eucharistic prayer should ring in our ears as continual reminders of what God does among us: "Again and again you gather a people to yourself. . . ." Those who pray comprise "the family you have gathered here before you."

There is a delicate balance in liturgy: divine initiative and human response, the action of God and the sanctification of humanity. How one "achieves" this is part and parcel of liturgy as an art and a craft (to paraphrase Walter Burghardt). But even then it is not about what *we* achieve but what God works among and through us.

I noted at the outset that liturgy is always paschal and always pastoral—the church's central action of salvation and sanctification. Let me conclude by saying that liturgy is both something that *we* do and something that *does us.* We trip this delicate balance at our peril. For me, this is a helpful juxtaposition that can help us retain appropriate serenity through some of the tensions surrounding liturgical revision, reform, and renewal. When liturgy's externals are overemphasized, we risk losing the heart of the matter: Liturgy is a privileged means toward the ends that only God can accomplish—to draw us into the very mystery of God through the liturgy wherein "the work of our salvation is accomplished."

NOTES

1. See, among others, Kevin W. Irwin, *Context and Text: Method in Liturgical Theology* (Collegeville, Minn.: Liturgical Press, 1994), Part 2.

2. For a helpful explanation of this approach to pastoral theology, see Karl Rahner, *Theology of Pastoral Action,* trans. W. J. O'Hara (New York: Herder and Herder, 1968).

3. In much of what follows this ecclesiological emphasis—as classical

as Saint Augustine and Saint Thomas Aquinas—will be presumed as well as emphasized.

4. For a helpful introduction to the usefulness of historical study for the liturgy, see Alexander Schmemann, *Introduction to Liturgical Theology* (London: The Faith Press, 1966).

5. See the Introduction and helpful collection of essays in Pierre-Marie Gy, *La Liturgie dans l'histoire* (Paris: Cerf, 1990).

6. For an ecumenical voice that presumes the value of the patristic era on other revised Christian liturgies, see Geoffrey Wainwright, *Worship with One Accord: Where Liturgy and Ecumenism Embrace* (New York and London: Oxford University Press, 1997).

7. For a popular overview regarding the Eucharist, see Edward Foley, *From Age to Age* (Chicago: Liturgy Training Publications, 1991).

8. As Robert Taft has argued in a recent address to the Society for Catholic Liturgy (September 1999), however, it must be admitted that at times elements of the Eastern liturgical tradition have been used for predetermined Western purposes, sometimes with mixed results.

9. See *General Instruction of the Roman Missal*, rev. ed. (2000), no. 78.

10. For an overview of some such voices see Kevin W. Irwin, "Critiquing Liturgical Critics," *Worship* (January 2000). Two of the clearest examples of this are Klaus Gamber, *The Reform of the Roman Liturgy: Its Problems and Background* (Harrison, N.Y.: Una Voce Press, 1993); and Catherine Pickstock, *After Writing: On the Liturgical Consummation of Philosophy* (Oxford: Blackwell, 1998).

11. For an example of an alternative reading of liturgical history, see Aidan Nichols, "A Historical Inquest," in *Looking at the Liturgy: A Critical View of Its Contemporary Form* (San Francisco: Ignatius Press, 1996), 11–148.

12. See Kevin W. Irwin, *Liturgical Theology: A Primer* (Collegeville, Minn.: Liturgical Press, 1990), 18–39 and bibliography.

13. Ibid., 40–47.

14. See the published papers from the meeting of the Societas Liturgica on the topic of liturgical theology held at Kottayam India (*Studia Liturgica* 30/1 [2000] and *La Maison Dieu* 221 [2000]).

15. See, among others, Regis Duffy, *The Liturgy and the Catechism: Celebrating God's Wisdom and Love* (London: Geoffrey Chapman, 1995).

16. See Robert J. Daly, "Robert Bellarmine and Post-Tridentine Eucharistic Theology," *Theological Studies* 61:2 (June 2000), 239–60.

17. See the last sections of each of the central chapters in Irwin, *Context and Text,* for indications of where ongoing revision and reform of the liturgy might be helpful.

18. See "The Milwaukee Symposia for Church Composers: A Ten Year Report" (9 July 1992) L. T. P. Publications, Chicago, and "The Snowbird Statement on Catholic Liturgical Music" (1 November 1995), the Madeline Institute, Salt Lake City, Utah.

19. See Irwin, *Context and Text*, 236–46.

20. For an overview of some particular challenges for liturgical architects today, see Richard S. Vosko, "A House for the Church: Structures for Public Worship in a New Millennium," *Worship* 74 (May 2000), 194–212.

21. For a helpful summary and overview of much of what is involved, see "Toward a Liturgical Aesthetic—An Interdisciplinary Review of Aesthetic Theory," *Liturgy Digest* 3:1 (1996), 4–144. Also see Albert Rouet, *Liturgy and the Arts*, trans. Paul Philibert (Collegeville, Minn.: Liturgical Press, 1997).

22. *General Instruction of the Roman Missal,* no. 78.

23. For the full text of the correspondence between Bishop David Foley and Cardinal Jorge Medina, see "Questions of Orthodoxy Regarding the New Order of Mass," *Antiphon* 5:1 (2000), 47–48.

24. See Cardinal Joseph Ratzinger, *The Spirit of the Liturgy,* trans. John Saward (San Francisco: Ignatius Press, 2000); see also Adoremus: Society for the Renewal of the Sacred Liturgy, *Adoremus Bulletin* 6:3 (May 2000).

25. See among others, Peter Jeffrey, *A New Commandment: Towards a Renewed Rite for the Washing of Feet* (Collegeville, Minn.: Liturgical Press, 1992); see also the Bishops' Committee on the Liturgy, "Women and the Holy Thursday Foot-Washing Ceremony," *Origins* 16 (19 March 1987), 712.

26. See Henri Denis, *Des sacrements et des hommes: Dix ans aprex Vatican II* (Lyons: Chalet, 1975); *Les sacrements ont-ils un avenir?* (Paris: Cerf, 1971); *Sacrements, Sources de vie: Etudes theologie sacramentaire* (Paris: Cerf, 1982); and Raymond Didier, *Les sacrements de la foi: La Paque sans ses signes* (Paris: Le Centurion, 1975).

27. See Adrien Nocent, *A Rereading of the Renewed Liturgy*, trans. Mary M. Misrahi (Collegeville, Minn.: Liturgical Press, 1994), 67–83.

28. See Marva J. Dawn, *Reaching Out Without Dumbing Down: A Theology of Worship for the Turn-of-the-Century Culture* (Grand Rapids, Mich.: Eerdmans, 1995); and idem, *A Royal "Waste" of Time: The Splendor of Worshiping God and Being Church for the World* (Grand Rapids, Mich.: Eerdmans, 1999).

CONCLUDING
REFLECTIONS

I. A Note on Vatican II in Historical Perspective

Monika K. Hellwig

It is good to be here, at this juncture of history, at this college, in this company and at this celebration! The forty years of the graduate theology program at St. Michael's College have been an extraordinary time in the history of the church, a time of reawakening of the church as people of God, a time of reawakening of the laity to an active role in the church and in the redemption of the world. And this graduate program has been a not insignificant actor in the process.

Forty years ago we were on the eve of the Second Vatican Council. In this country there was much stirring. The Sister Formation Movement was beginning a revolution in consciousness, competence, and roles. It was a gathering tide that could never be reversed, sweeping a great deal of debris and wreckage out of the way and making way for new beginnings. At the University of Notre Dame in the summer school of liturgy the great European theologians—most of them then under a cloud but later architects of Vatican II—were sowing their ideas in the minds of hundreds of graduate students each year. At Marquette University and elsewhere a keen realization was taking hold that religious courses for college students should be neither catechesis nor seminary manual imitations but something quite different, challenging, critical, and creative in matters pertinent both to the present experience and to the future lives of the students. And on the eve of the council programs such as this one began to open the gates wider to layfolk hungry for deeper understanding and deeper engagement in their Christian faith.

These four decades have seen a breaking open of the scriptures for the people of God in ways that had not happened within the Catholic Church for long centuries. These have been decades of rediscovering our spirituality traditions, decades of liturgical blossoming, decades of a whole new and expanded sense of the social justice concerns integral to the lived gospel of Jesus Christ. In the blast of the "New Pentecost" we have rediscovered our identity as church with a mission in the world, church defined by inclusion not exclusion, church truly present and active in the real events and challenges of history. All this required Catholics not only committed to the pursuit of the reign of God but truly understanding what is involved in that pursuit. It required biblically, liturgically, and theologically formed adults with a strong sense of community and mission. And this is what programs such as this one at St. Michael's have contributed.

Of course, this has not been like a triumphal march, a simple forward progression of a church with shared vision and purpose. It brought almost immediately a reaction from the Roman Curia, which had indeed bitterly opposed much of what happened in the council itself. The reaction was one of new efforts to centralize and control everything. We have seen efforts to control language in the liturgy, in Bible translations, in instruction, and so forth. We have seen efforts to curtail the freedom of bishops and bishops' conferences to teach and to speak according to their own pastoral discernment. We have seen efforts to assert canonical control over freestanding institutions such as hospitals and universities and colleges. There has been a concerted attack on the exercise and even the naming of lay ministry. And there have been the fiercest efforts to control the use of the "trademark"—the word *Catholic*—guarded like a royal seal.

There have been two sets of reasons for this reaction from the Curia. One is easy to see and to understand, namely, that not all innovation, adaptation, and experimentation has been prudent. There have been indiscretions and abuses that were bound to alert and concern the relevant authorities. But a more fundamental set of reasons lies in the conflict, unresolved in the documents of the Second Vatican Council, between two quite different concepts of ecclesiology. They are roughly equivalent to the second and third chapters of the dogmatic constitution *Lumen gentium.*

The dominant note of the Second Vatican Council (*LG,* chap. II) is the call of the people of God in pilgrimage to the reign of God. This is a dynamic image, implying change, striving forward, creative human activity, energy rising from the ranks, a prophetic calling. In this image the divine element of the church is the person of Jesus Christ from which it takes its origin and inspiration, the Spirit that is always with the followers of Jesus as they meet the various challenges and exigencies of the centuries and the nations, and the transcendent God who is always in the future calling. The human element in this image includes all the structures and formulations accumulated through the ages as we have tried to embody the vision and the ideal—structures like the organiza- tion of church governance, the Code of Canon Law, the patterns of sacramental worship, the various catechisms and theological manuals and conciliar definitions.

The other note (*LG,* chap. III), which the curial cardinals and bish- ops at Vatican II continue to see as the real theology of the church, is the establishment of the age-old and unchanging rock of Peter. And Peter is interpreted as including the entire elaborate bureaucracy of the present- day Curia, including all the claims to authority that curial officials have made on their own initiative, most of them since the nineteenth century. On this ecclesiological basis, what Jesus left us was this whole elaborate church structure, even though some of it only unfolded in the course of the centuries. And on this understanding the fidelity in discipleship means above all keeping the structure intact in every detail, bringing as many people as possible into the Catholic Church, keeping them there, and making sure all Catholics are properly subordinated to those struc- tures and rules. With such presuppositions it is more than reasonable to resist trends toward spontaneity, assertions of the principle of subsidiar- ity, the concept of collegiality, and any focus on the autonomy of local churches in their own pastoral discernment.

Where has this polarity in ecclesiology left us? In other words, how are we to interpret the situation in which we are in the present time? It is undeniable that we are in a time of sharp tensions, and that for all of us who are in various church ministries it is therefore an uncomfortable time. It is a time of polarization of leadership, though that seems for the time being to leave great numbers of faithful Catholics untouched or at least untroubled by the very vocal, though very small, minorities. For some, it has been a time of discouragement and departure, while for others it continues to be a time of hope. Certainly, it is a time both of great possibilities and of great risks. The most serious risks seem to be those of schisms and those of quiet discouragement and withdrawal from more active involvement. Neither of these is evident in this gathering where the enthusiasm of Vatican II is very much alive today. And for this we must be very grateful to God and to those who built the program and dedicated their energies to it.

In a gathering like this, therefore, one may ask seriously not only where we are but where we ought to be going. My foremost thought on where we ought to be going is that we need urgently to be concerned with a deeper appropriation of the intellectual and cultural heritage of Catholicism. In the decades since Vatican II we have greatly improved Catholic knowledge of the Bible, both acquaintance with the text and understanding of how to interpret it. We have also greatly improved and expanded our ecumenical relations with other Christians, both in practice and in knowledge and understanding of their traditions. And we have ventured in many good ways into the wider ecumenism of knowing and understanding the other religions of the world. We have come to a better understanding of conscience formation as involving far more than memorization of rules. And we have become aware of the need to explore the nature of religious language and of faith as well as the inescapable historicity and cultural particularity of all formulations. All this has been necessary, long overdue in Catholic church circles, and excellent. But in our rapid efforts to catch up with the four centuries of development in the world since the Council of Trent, what we have not been able to do is to lay a sufficient foundation of solid acquaintance with our own tradition in all its riches. On this we need to focus in planning for the future.

A necessary element of such appropriation of the intellectual and cultural tradition is a much greater concern with history than we have put to work in the past, even in the recent past. There are two aspects to this. First there is the far more thorough acquaintance with what has actually happened in our community, as that information is available from the more trustworthy contemporary witnesses. The importance of this lies in the fact that knowing how rules, doctrines, structures of governance, and so forth developed is the key to having a good sense of what is of permanent worth and what is transitory, what is authentic development and what is distortion, what is essential and what is accidental. We are in an era when such discernment is crucial, because we are in a world of rapid change in all dimensions of human experience. But the concern with history has another aspect, and that is the appreciation of the historicity of everything, the understanding that past events must be interpreted in their own context, that language changes constantly so that verbal orthodoxy may be the greatest betrayal of the original intent, and that structures and rules supportive of a purpose in one context may subvert it in another context. We have made great strides in the appreciation of historicity but often with inadequate knowledge of the history itself.

Another concern that seems to me urgent and basic is the uncovering and acknowledgement of the implicit ecclesiologies with which we are all working, and which often come to be a hidden agenda in practical disagreements over local or universal church affairs, as in questions of social-justice activity in the name of gospel and church and in questions concerning roles and ministries within the church itself. Moreover, the implicit ecclesiologies are intertwined with implicit soteriologies. These last may start from such widely divergent, but unacknowledged, assumptions as to lead dedicated Christians to see one another as deluded, as destroyers of church and faith, as veritable anti-Christs. It is important to explore these hidden foundations for the often heated disagreements within the church community.

The last concern that I want to mention here is perhaps a more subtle one. Because we are in a time of rapid and disputed changes, a time that is necessarily one of some bewilderment and uncertainty, it seems to me that it is more important than ever to be absolutely, even ruthlessly, honest with ourselves about what is understood and what remains a question, about what fits coherently in our understanding and what is out of harmony with our new understanding. In the Catholic Church context we have not been very good at admitting what we do not know or cannot make sense of. We have inherited too slick and self-assured a comprehensive set of answers and explanations. What we inherited was coherent enough in a philosophical, cultural, and scientific thought-world in which we are no longer at home. Again and again the questions that arise out of our contemporary experience shoot right out of the framework of that tidy system that held together our inherited account of our beliefs. We cannot possibly have a completely coherent new account at a time of such rapid change in philosophy, culture, and science. We need to make the effort at coherence, but I think we also need to be totally honest about never quite achieving it.

What I think this graduate program has done over the decades of its existence is to open many doors and windows, to give some good indications of the various directions one might take in pursuit of the reign of God, and then to propel its students into fully adult responsibilities in the faith—responsibilities to search on one's own, to keep becoming more fully informed, to be faithful to the quest for understanding and coherence, and to maintain fellowship and community with others who are honestly searching. And that is the achievement and the glory of the program, for which we thank all who have participated in it, and encourage all who do and will participate in it.

II. Catholic Theology: Contextual, Historical, Inventive

Terrence W. Tilley

Four days of remarkably stimulating reflection on the past, present, and future of Catholic theology leaves me enriched, humbled, and enthused. Enriched by the remarkable presentations—nuanced, provocative, precise reflections on where we have been as a people of God over the last forty years.[1] Humbled by the sheer intellectual and communicative power of my distinguished and modest colleagues, who have been more comprehensive, lucid, and challenging than I thought possible. Enthused for our future together, for we see how much we have to do to keep theology living and faithful in the future and how much hope there is that we shall be able to continue to serve. To say that these days have been stimulating is to say that we have been graced by God to work in the re-creation of the tradition we love.[2]

Attempting to summarize is impossible. I would, however, like to share with you three key themes that I find running through the presentations. These themes are more explicit in some chapters than in others, of course. And other commentators would highlight other themes—there are many paths we could follow through this material. I summarize them with pithy mottos so you will remember them: *Always Contextualize, Always Historicize,* and *Always Invent.*

ALWAYS CONTEXTUALIZE

In the very first chapter Dermot Lane said that theology is always local. Theology is done from a certain place and in a certain time. Whether it is done in the catacombs or the desert, in the monastery or the medieval university, in the chapter house or the seminary, in the small basic community or the modern research university, no theology has a "God's eye-view," a "view from nowhere." Even if theology's hands reach for the Infinite, theology's feet are firmly planted in the theologian's specific social location. Theology may be done *for* the whole people of God, but it originates *from* specific local incarnations of that multi-generational community.

To understand a theological position or claim, then, we must always contextualize it. We must know when and where it was formulated. We must know the challenges to which a theologian or a council or a pope responded. We must know the purposes for the responses. We must know the options really available and not taken (for we may have possibilities they did not and they may have had possibilities we do not).[3] An uncontextualized theological claim is empty—How could one possibly say what it meant apart from any sort of context in which it was issued?

Repeating a theological formula is never a guarantee of religious continuity or fidelity. No theological formula can retain an utter stability of meaning through translations, profound cultural changes, and the evolution of languages. We can never simply transliterate formulas to understand our tradition; we always must interpret the "old creeds" in the "new world."[4] We must interpret the tradition developed in other contexts by transforming it for a new context—ours! Our successors will then interpret and transform what we say for their contexts.

Some think the work of contextualization is finished when one locates the specific social location of the speaker—race, gender, class, nationality, ecclesial status, and so forth.[5] This is, however, only the beginning of the work. For contextualization includes not only the speaker but also the speaker's audience, the community that the speaker serves. It also includes specific *religious* trends—not merely social or cultural trends—that are important for understanding the context in which theologians work.

Today, we must pay special attention to our community. Two factors—highlighted especially by Alice Laffey—are important. First, we are a multi-cultural, multi-ethnic, multi-racial community. On an ordinary Sunday, for instance, Mass is celebrated in over thirty languages in the Archdiocese of Los Angeles. More than 50 percent of Catholics will be Hispanic-Latino/a in a few years (and we must take care not to lump their cultures together; Cuban-Americans and Mexican-Americans have very different cultural contexts). We can no longer presume a context of monoculturalism or ignore the diversity in our church. Our community is a diverse one. Second, we are deeply affected by generational differences. As Alice Laffey, learning as I have from James D. Davidson, points out, there are profound religious and attitudinal differences among "pre–Vatican II Catholics" (those whose religious formation was essentially complete by the time Vatican II started), "Vatican II Catholics" (those whose religious formation was strongly affected by Vatican II and the other challenging events and movements of the turbulent sixties), and "post–Vatican II Catholics" (those whose religious formation began after Vatican II ended; for them, Vatican II is not a "memory" but something found in history books). I will not reiterate here the shifts that Davidson discovers and Laffey reports. Yet one factor stands out. For the pre–Vatican II Catholics, Catholicism was predominantly something given to them and to which they conformed (or not). For the Vatican II Catholics, historic Catholicism was something they were given and which was being profoundly reformed (for better or worse). For post–Vatican II Catholics, Catholicism is an option that they may or may not choose to exercise. In their era, to be a Catholic is voluntary, and the church now has the social characteristics of a voluntary society.

The differences are crucial. Earlier Catholics were made by their religious traditions. More recent Catholics make their own religion. We can say that the concept of religious freedom moved from the political to the personal, psychological realm in this era. Similarly, pursuing one's own spiritual quest is no longer a practice only for the elite but is now the pattern for every individual—so much so that spiritual self-help and guide books become best-sellers.

Theology done in the present context cannot parrot theologies done in other contexts. While remaining faithful to the tradition, we must learn ways to theologize in, for, and from the present context. While "always contextualize" may be a motto, its purpose is not only to urge certain theological strategies, but also to remind us that all theology is contextual and needs to be treated as contingent expressions of eternal truths. No one has the whole truth yet—except God, and even God must communicate whatever eternal truths there are in temporal terms.

ALWAYS HISTORICIZE

Some would treat this motto as merely derivative from the previous one. And for some purposes, those folk would be right. However, for those to whom fidelity to a tradition is a paramount value, historical study is an utter necessity, not merely to "contextualize" the past, but also to "relativize" the present, and to keep hope alive for the future.

Catholics are members of a mystical body, of a communion of saints. Where we are as Christians is determined, in part, by where we, as a Christian community, have been. Where we can go as Christians is determined, in part, by what possibilities we can see in the future for the life of our community. If we would know who we are and where we want to go, we must know the past of where we have been and imagine the futures into which we may emerge.

Historicizing is "deabsolutizing"; it is relativizing. But lest this be thought to be a weakness, let me urge you to think of it as a strength. A "default setting" of human consciousness is to think that the past was like the present, that the way things are is the way things have always been. Comic strips frequently poke fun at this view. Dennis the Menace, for example, cannot imagine Mr. Wilson's youth without television. Like all of us, Dennis thinks the past must be like the present. To think of Mr. Wilson's childhood is, for Dennis, to try to think the unthinkable. History teaches us that the present is not absolute, that the trials and triumphs, the tragedies and the glories, the hopes and fears of the present are not necessarily the way things have been, must be, or ought be. My own teacher, the late Msgr. John Tracy Ellis, frequently reminded his students that "this, too, shall pass," that the church of the immediate present was bound to change, for "she always had in the past and will in the future." History leaves us room for hope; we learn that the future does not have to be like the past because the present is not just like the past.

Those who historicize all claims know how liberating the doing and study of history can be for a people committed to a tradition. Carried to an extreme, historicization can lead to the anarchy of historicism and relativism. But its opposite can lead even more easily to the tyranny of intellectual absolutism and ecclesial totalitarianism. The key is to know how the monuments of the past point us in a certain direction but do not instruct us how we are to get to our goal—life eternally with God.

For some of us, knowing that the church of the future will not be like the church that raised us up is discouraging. Certainly post–Vatican II Catholics and the theologians that they are producing have different styles and concerns from those of my generation. But this is true of every generation, and we simply must accept the reality of change and even the goodness of it in God's plan.

ALWAYS INVENT

The challenge we face today is to invent a Catholic tradition worth passing to our children and for them to find worth passing to their children. Tradition is not a *thing* we pass on but the *practice* of passing on. Yes, I do intend the allusion—a living tradition requires the death of the sacred past and a resurrection into a future of hope. As I suggested earlier, fidelity to the tradition cannot be parroting the past. While being faithful to the past, the future is ours and our successors' to invent.[6] What we must do, though, is first not to obstruct ourselves.

Three aphorisms can help us avoid this sort of self-obstruction. First, If you know what is true, you cannot seek what is true. Those who "know it all" obstruct the quest for knowledge and wisdom because they have nowhere they need to go. Second, If you are certain something is true, you cannot hope that it is true. In fancy language, hoping and being certain are incompatible epistemic attitudes. Certainty is the end of hope. Third, If you are not suffering, you don't need and can't have hope. For if you lack nothing, what can you hope for?

We can no longer do theology as we did even a quarter century ago. We can no longer talk of that imaginary figure, "modern man" [*sic*] and "his" [*sic*] concerns. Today, for Catholic theology to live, theologians must work contextually, be historically informed, and be ready to invent a future in which the past (including the past that we become) is neither ignored and forgotten nor made the object of stultifying nostalgia, but in which our shared past is both our heritage and God's joy.

As we have heard, the last forty years have been a time of suffering and joy, of challenge and hope, of loss and gain. But, "'twas ever thus," and always will be, this side of eternity. God willing, in a new context and a new time and place, Catholicism will be true to itself and reinvent itself. For life goes on. . . .

Thanks be to God.

NOTES

1. Although this essay is written from notes used at the reunion's concluding session, it is not a close approximation of what was said there but a reflection on the themes developed in a way that tries to retain the spirit of the *ex tempore* oral presentation.

2. This rather strong claim reflects my understanding of the transmission of tradition (see Terrence W. Tilley, *Inventing Catholic Tradition* [Maryknoll, N.Y.: Orbis Books, 2000]).

3. For a fine example of understanding through contextualization, see Francis A. Sullivan, S.J., *Salvation Outside the Church?: Tracing the History of the Catholic Response* (New York: Paulist Press, 1992). Although the evidence is not conclusive, there is good reason to think that Sullivan's work influenced the important 1997 document of the International Theological Commission, "Christianity and the World Religions," *Origins* 27/10 (14 August 1997).

4. This alludes to the public profession of faith "Old Creeds in a New World" given by Secretary General Dag Hammarskjöld in April 1953.

5. "Speaker" also includes "writer." While there are important differences between them, both speaking and writing are communicative actions and can be combined in the present context.

6. It is important to note that this is not a task for individuals. Communities made the past, and communities of people will invent the future. While an individual may be the occasion for the new in Christ to change the old world, inventing and reinventing a tradition is a shared project.

III. Let's Begin—Not End— Theology with Hope

Dermot A. Lane

By way of conclusion I would like to say something about a subject that has been hovering around these contributions, namely, hope. It is, of course, inevitable at the end of a stimulating conference that expressions of hope should be sounded. The issue of hope, however, is more central to theology than simply a statement of positive sentiment. I have misgivings about references to hope that do not say something about the meaning and content of hope. Further, hope at the end may come too late to be effective within the proceedings. Similarly, hope at the end is too vague to be enduring. The idea of "concluding reflections" offers an opportunity to redress this problem in some small way.

There has been a persistent tendency within theology simply to add hope, almost as an afterthought, to the end of the Christian reflection and praxis. This, of course, has a number of unhappy and undesirable consequences. Foremost among these is a presentation of hope as something bland and bloodless. Probably the most serious consequence of leaving hope to the end is the neutralization and marginalization of hope within theology. To be sure Jürgen Moltmann and Johann B. Metz sought in the middle sixties to bring hope into the center of the theological stage—but their important contributions have had mixed results.

SOME REASONS FOR BEGINNING THEOLOGY WITH HOPE

I propose that a strong case exists for beginning the whole of theology with hope. There are a number of compelling reasons prompting this proposal. Looking back over the twentieth century, it is quite remarkable how faith, hope, and love have become separated and isolated from each other. Faith without hope is in danger of becoming an ideology, and love without hope can become self-indulgent or simply sentimental. If it is true to say in the aftermath of the Enlightenment that unbelief has been one of the key issues for theology in the twentieth century, it now seems true to say in the light of so much apathy today that hope will be one of the key questions facing humanity and theology at the beginning of this new century. The real issue for theology today is how to effect a new organic unity among faith, hope, and love in a way that can be brought to bear on the whole of the theological enterprise. As Karl Rahner frequently pointed out, we do not really know who God is and who we are until we begin to hope.

Another reason theology should begin with hope is the growing awareness of the importance of ecological issues and the need to link ecology and theology. Such noble concerns, however, appear as empty rhetoric unless they are anchored in the praxis of Christian hope directed to the pain of the earth. It is now clearly established that the well-being of the earth is bound up with the well-being of humanity and this in itself is a good reason for redrawing the boundaries of a theology of hope so as to embrace the individual, society, and the cosmos.

A third reason hope should become the point of departure for theology is that important links exist between anthropology and hope. To hope is to be human, and every human being lives, either tacitly or explicitly, out of hope. A theology that begins with hope will be a theology that sets out to describe from the beginning what it means to be human. This concern about what it means to be human, and what it is that we hope for, could give theology a more inclusive point of departure.

A fourth reason theology should begin with hope is that this will bring out the practical character of Christianity. Important links exist between the act of hope and the praxis of individual and social transformation. In an important sense I hope what I do and I do what I hope. One of the primary tasks facing theology is to be able to give an account of the hope that is in us in terms of the practical difference it makes to live lives of hope. If this cannot be done, then Marx's critique of religion as "the opium of the people" and Nietzsche's charge that Christianity is a "world-denying Platonism" remain in place.

IS HOPE POSSIBLE WITHIN A CULTURE OF POSTMODERNITY?

In making this proposal for a hope-centered theology and a more unified relationship among hope, faith, and love throughout theology, we must give at least some broad indication of what this suggestion implies. Context, of course, is always important. As noted in Chapter 1, theology finds itself caught between the ambiguous advances of modernity and the destructive acids of postmodernity. Modernity with its pervasive myth of progress has pushed hope to the margins of theology and replaced it with secular optimism. It is increasingly clear, however, that this optimism of modernity is now bankrupt, and this, it might be argued, creates a new opening for hope.

When we turn to postmodernity we are informed that one of the first casualties arising out of its radical program of deconstruction is that of eschatology, and that therefore there is very little room for hope within the culture of postmodernity. For example, Mark C. Taylor believes that the deconstruction by postmodernity of meta-narrative, history, and anthropology necessitates the elimination of eschatology. Taylor writes: "The death of Alpha and Omega, the disappearance of the self and the overcoming of unhappy consciousness combine to fray the fabric of history. When it is impossible to locate a definite beginning and a definite end, the narrative line is lost and the story seems pointless."[1] Given this outlook life takes on what Taylor honestly describes as an "unavoidable purposelessness."[2] These negative comments against the possibility of hope within a postmodern framework force us to ask: What is hope, how does hope function, and what are its sources?

Paul Ricoeur, as far back as 1970, tells us that hope is a protest against the premature closure of systems; that hope keeps thought open; that hope reacts against all claims to absolute knowledge, especially the transcendental illusion of absolute knowledge or indeed the dialectic that produces rationalistic reconciliations. Hope, therefore, is not so much an object alongside other objects, not a theme coming after all other themes, not an idea arriving at the end that closes the system. Instead, hope is an impulse that breaks open the system, radically resists the closure of thought, and recognizes the limits attaching to human systems.

Ricoeur assures us that this view of hope does have its own peculiar kind of intelligibly (*intellectus spei*). The refusal of hope to concede the closure of human thought contains elements of irrationality and intelligibility. The irrationality of hope is found in the movement forward in the face of failure and suffering as well as darkness and death. Hope does not turn its back on these negative realities of life; instead, hope faces the future deeply conscious of the negative. At the same time, it takes this step forward on the basis of the excess of sense over non-sense and meaningfulness over meaninglessness as well as the presence of an abundance in life that is given in nature, history, and human creativity. It is the existence of these elements of excess and abundance that sources the intelligibility peculiar to hope.[3] Hope, if it is to be taken seriously, requires reason, but if reason is to flourish, it requires hope (*spero ut intelligam*). Ricoeur is talking here primarily about a philosophy of hope, even though much of what he has to say about a philosophy of hope could also apply to a theology of hope, with some further nuances that we will touch on presently.

What is fascinating about this preliminary account of hope is the echo that exists between it and the underlying ideas informing some proponents of postmodernity. As noted in Chapter 1, postmodernity is a program of radical deconstruction: the deconstruction of meta-narratives, history, modern certainties, and the human self. Much of postmodernity appears destructive, relativistic, and ultimately nihilistic, at least at first glance. The question, however, that must be asked is this: What is it that drives this program of deconstruction, what is the source of this radical critique, what motivates postmodernity to say no to everything?

In response to these questions Jacques Derrida talks about the messianic structure of human experience. By this he means that built into human experience there is a strong sense of expectation and promise, an ancient promise that "performs (and pre-forms) us before we perform it."[4] In particular, Derrida talks about the possibility of the impossible, a passion for justice, an openness to the future and all that is coming. Even Jean-François Lyotard claims that postmoderns are called "to be witnesses to unpresentable."[5]

If we compare Ricoeur's philosophy of hope with this postmodern "philosophy" of deconstruction, we find close parallels between hope and the deconstruction of postmodernity. These parallels are so close that it seems reasonable to suggest that some of the deconstruction of postmodernity is driven by hope, even though this hope is extremely vague. Surely a concern for the other, preoccupation with the possibility of the impossible, a passion for justice, a sense of expectation and promise, an openness to the future and all that is coming are closely connected to the subject of hope.

A real difference does exists, however, between Ricoeur's philosophy of hope and the hope of postmodernity in that postmoderns refuse to admit or concede any mediation or manifestation of hope in nature, history, or human experience. Postmoderns also deny the realization of any messianic expectation in history or the fulfillment of justice. What is important here, from our limited point of view, is to note the common ground that exists within a philosophy of hope as outlined by Ricoeur and the hope implicit in the deconstruction of postmodernity. To begin theology with hope, therefore, will engage theology from the outset not only with what is most fundamental to the human condition but also with all who would seek to deconstruct theology.

THE VISION AND CONTENT OF HOPE

If hope is about resistance to the status quo and a protest against the closure of human thought—and I do think that this is the proper point of departure for a theology of hope—then it becomes equally urgent for a theology of hope to articulate some vision and content for hope, no matter how provisional or penultimate this vision and content may be.

For example, Michael J. Scanlon asks the question "What can we hope for" and notes two quite distinct and different answers found among most Christians.[6] Some reply, eternal life after death for the purified soul, whereas others hope for a more peaceful order in the present *and* eternal life in the future. For too long Christian hope has appeared to be solely spiritual, otherworldly, and futuristic, that is, ahistorical, apolitical, and disembodied. The time has come, especially in the light of the biblical recovery of the eschatology of Jesus (*pace* the U.S. Jesus seminar) and the teaching of the Second Vatican Council (especially in *Gaudium et spes*), to see Christian hope as this worldly *and* otherworldly, as embracing the present *and* the future, as integrating the spiritual *and* the social.

When this more inclusive approach to a theology of hope takes place, then Christian hope can begin to assume a greater social and ecological responsibility, without, however, reducing the object of hope simply to the level of the purely immanent. It is, of course, essential in any theology of hope to remind ourselves that it is God who effects salvation in this life and in the world to come. At the same time, however, the life of hope is an invitation to participate in God's project of the coming reign of God for humanity in the present and the future. It is within this more holistic approach to a theology of hope that we can see the full force of the now famous lines of the Irish poet Seamus Heaney:

> History says, *Don't hope*
> *On this side of the grave.*
> But then, once in a lifetime
> The longed-for tidal wave
> Of justice can rise up,
> And hope and history rhyme.[7]

The longed-for tidal wave has already risen up in the mission and ministry of Jesus as the Christ. It now remains for the disciples of Jesus to keep that tidal wave active in the church and society.

Mention of the mission and ministry of Jesus requires us also to say something, however brief, about the theological significance of the cross and resurrection of Jesus for hope. It is the death and resurrection of Jesus as the Christ of God that is the centerpiece of Christian hope. The crucified and risen Christ is the hope of the world and, as such, gives direction to Christian hope that can only be very briefly summarized here.

The *shape* of Christian hope is cruciform. The future, both individually and collectively, is marked with the sign of the cross. There is no way around the vulnerable, finite, and mortal character of human existence. Christian hope does not ignore the flawed aspects of life; instead, it sees light in the brokenness of Jesus on the cross; it is above all else the stark reality of the cross that is the most potent symbol of hope for Christian faith.

The *rhythm* of Christian hope is paschal: dying and rising, decentering and recentering the self, passing over to the other and returning transformed. Some of this paschal rhythm is capture by Emily Dickinson in her striking lines:

> A death-blow is a life-blow to some
> Who 'till they died, did not alive become,
> Who had they lived, had died but when
> They died, vitality begun.[8]

This creative unity of living and dying, the integration of death and life, is the potent meaning and message of the historical death and resurrection of Jesus for hope.

The *color* of Christian hope is that of a "bright darkness." The realism of Christian hope requires that we acknowledge the existence of darkness and death in life but at the same time refuses to allow them to have the last word. Instead, Christian hope is able to see light in the darkness and life in death. An example of this paradox can be found in the image of a statue that has a hairline fracture. The fracture can only be overcome through a process of breaking down the statue into its raw material in order to recover its original beauty. Something similar happens to the human being who in death undergoes disintegration so that there can be reintegration into God. In this sense Christian hope embraces a "bright darkness" and a joy tinged with sadness.

And finally, the *outcome* of Christian hope is some form of transformed embodied existence. Christianity is a "material" religion, and therefore it claims that future existence, both individual and cosmic, embraces bodiliness transformed. If scientists can talk about the human self as cosmic dust come alive in human form, why cannot Christians claim that the dust of the dead becomes a new creation in Christ? The Christian doctrines of the Incarnation and the Resurrection of the body, each in its own way, point toward God's adoption of the material universe as part not only of history but also of eternity.

In short, Christian hope assures us that in the darkness of death we fall not into emptiness but into the fullness of new life, not into the black holes of outer space but into the glory of eternity, not into the abyss of nothingness but into the depth of everlasting communion in the triune God.

NOTES

1. M. C. Taylor, *Erring: A Postmodern A/Theology* (Chicago: University of Chicago Press, 1984), 73.

2. Ibid., 157.

3. Paul Ricoeur, "Hope and the Structure of Philosophical Systems," *Proceedings of the American Catholic Association* (1970), 55–69.

4. John D. Caputo, *The Prayers and Tears of Jacques Derrida: Religion without Religion* (Bloomington, Ind.: Indiana University Press, 1977), 31.

5. Jean-François Lyotard, *The Postmodern Condition* (Manchester: Manchester University Press, 1986), 82.

6. Michael Scanlon, "Hope," in *The New Dictionary of Theology*, ed. Joseph A. Komonchak (Wilmington, Del.: Glazier, 1987), 497.

7. Seamus Heaney, *The Curé at Troy: A Version of Sophocles' Philoctetes* (London: Faber and Faber/Field Day, 1990), 77, emphasis added.

8. Emily Dickinson, "Part Four: Time and Eternity."

Contributors

Raymond F. Collins is a priest of the Diocese of Providence. From 1970 to 1993 he was Professor of New Testament Studies at the Catholic University of Leuven, and from 1993 to 1999 he served as Dean of the School of Religious Studies at the Catholic University of America. His books include *Preaching the Epistles; First Corinthians;* and *Sexual Ethics and the New Testament.*

Michael A. Fahey is Jesuit Professor of Theology at Marquette University and Editor-in-Chief of *Theological Studies*. He specializes in ecclesiology and ecumenism. He is a former president of the Catholic Theological Society of America. He has published several books, including *Trinitarian Theology East and West* and *Catholic Perspectives on Baptism, Eucharist, and Ministry.*

Monika K. Hellwig has served as the Executive Director of the Association of Catholic Colleges and Universities since 1966. She is a past president of the Catholic Theological Society of America. She has been awarded more than twenty honorary doctorate degrees from Catholic colleges and universities, including St. Michael's College in 1986.

Kevin W. Irwin is Professor of Liturgy and Sacramental Theology at the Catholic University of America, Washington D.C. He is widely published in various theological journals and has authored several books, including *Context and Text: Method in Liturgical Theology* and *Liturgical Theology: A Primer.*

Philip S. Keane is a Sulpician and Professor of Moral Theology at St. Mary's Seminary and University in Baltimore. His books include *Sexual Morality: A Catholic Perspective; Christian Ethics and Imagination;* and *Health Care Reform: A Catholic View.* He serves as a medical ethics consultant to the Maryland Catholic Health Care Consortium and several Catholic hospitals.

Alice L. Laffey is Associate Professor of Old Testament at the College of the Holy Cross, Worcester, Massachusetts. She has published several monographs, including *The Pentateuch: Liberation-Critical Reading* and *Appreciating God's Creation Through Scripture* and various commentaries for the Collegeville Bible Commentary Series.

Dermot A. Lane is President of Mater Dei Institute of Education in Dublin and serves as parish priest at the Church of the Ascension. He has edited and written several books. Recently he authored *Keeping Hope Alive: Stirrings in Christian Theology* and edited *New Century, New Society: Christian Reflections.*

Terrence W. Tilley is Professor and Chairperson in the Department of Religious Studies at the University of Dayton in Ohio. Prior to his appointment at Dayton, he taught at Florida State University, St. Michael's College, and Georgetown University. His most recent publication is *Inventing Catholic Tradition.* He has served as president of the College Theology Society and as a board member of the Catholic Theological Society of America.

Index